ROBERT WARREN'S
guide to painting
water
scenes

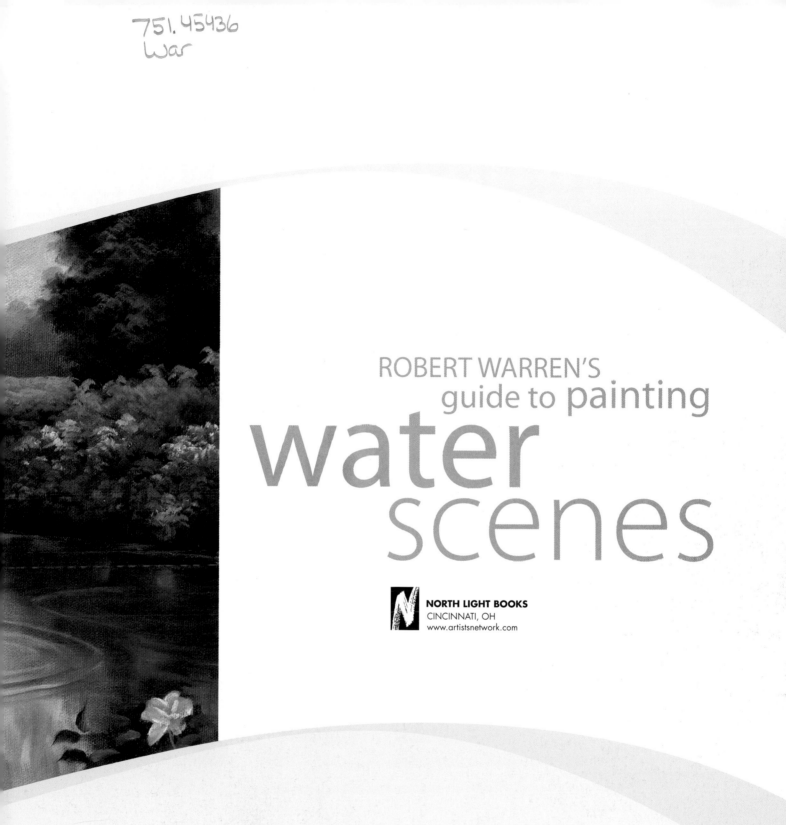

ROBERT WARREN'S
guide to painting

water
scenes

NORTH LIGHT BOOKS
CINCINNATI, OH
www.artistsnetwork.com

fw
F+W PUBLICATIONS, INC.

Other fine North Light Books are available from your local bookstore, art supply store or direct from the publisher.

10 09 08 07 06   5 4 3 2 1

Distributed in Canada by Fraser Direct, 100 Armstrong Avenue, Georgetown, ON, Canada L7G 5S4, Tel: (905) 877-4411

Distributed in the U.K. and Europe by David & Charles, Brunel House, Newton Abbot, Devon, TQ12 4PU, England Tel: (+44) 1626 323200, Fax: (+44) 1626 323319, Email: postmaster@davidandcharles.co.uk

Distributed in Australia by Capricorn Link, P.O. Box 704, S. Windsor NSW, 2756 Australia, Tel: (02) 4577-3555

Library of Congress Cataloging-in-Publication Data

Warren, Robert.
    Robert Warren's guide to painting water scenes / Robert Warren. -- 1st ed.
        p. cm.
    Includes index.
    ISBN-13: 978-1-58180-851-3 (pbk. : alk. paper)
    ISBN-10: 1-58180-851-8 (pbk. : alk. paper)
    1. Water in art. 2. Painting--Technique. I. Title. II. Title: Guide to painting water scenes.
ND1460.W39W37 2007
751.45'436--dc22

                        2006011256

Editor: Holly Davis
Production Coordinator: Greg Nock
Designer: Clare Finney
Interior Layout Artist: Jessica Schultz
Photographer: Christine Polomsky

METRIC CONVERSION CHART

to convert	to	multiply by
Inches	Centimeters	2.54
Centimeters	Inches	0.4
Feet	Centimeters	30.5
Centimeters	Feet	0.03
Yards	Meters	0.9
Meters	Yards	1.1

About the Author

Robert Warren has been a professional artist for more than 30 years. Although greatly influenced by his mentor and dear friend, the late William Alexander, his ala prima style of painting and teaching has been self-taught and his style has greatly evolved and developed over the span of his career.

Robert opened his current studio, Robert Warren's Art Loft, in Canal Winchester, Ohio, in 1986. He teaches monthly seminars and classes from beginning through advanced levels to students from around the country and the world. He has produced more than 200 instructional art shows for Alexander Art, Inc. and the Martin/ F. Weber company. "The Art of Robert Warren" has been broadcast worldwide for over 15 years on numerous cable and Public Broadcasting Stations. He has also authored nine instructional books.

Robert's website, www.RobertWarren ArtLoft.com, includes his gallery pieces, schedules of classes, and supplies, DVDs, or instructional material available for purchase.

Dedication

I would like to dedicate this book to my wife, Donna, and our artistic children Amanda, Robin, and Shawn for their limitless love and support through many years of enduring my artistic endeavors. I would also like to dedicate this to my mother, Vera Warren, who taught me great determination and provided me with the encouragement since childhood to continue my artistic journey. Last, I would like to thank my many loyal students who over a period of 30 years have encouraged and challenged me to grow. My hope is that I have touched your life as profoundly as you have mine.

Acknowledgments

Throughout any successful career, there are always those special individuals that have driven us with the fuel of inspiration. By combining inspiration and determination with a shot of confidence, a skill is developed and a passion is born. I would like to take this opportunity to acknowledge some of the most influential people in my artistic career: Jean Dodson, my art teacher from elementary through high school. Through her encouragement, I decided to major in art in college.

Dante Vena, Ph.D., my favorite and very inspiring college art professor at Ohio University. He recently retired as the head of the art department at the University of Massachusetts, but is still going strong.

My sister Lea Myles, who also became a renowned artist after getting acquainted with William Alexander and insisted that I meet this eccentric man with so much enthusiasm for life and painting. In fact, it was Lea who wrote and coordinated the first televised "how-to" oil painting programs with William Alexander. Many of today's television artists owe her a debt of gratitude for introducing this new media to millions of viewers.

My dear friend, the late William Alexander, my biggest source of artistic inspiration. He taught me to make art fun and the rewards of sharing my passion with others. Although my style has drastically changed from the "big mountains and pine tree paintings" that Bill was known for, I still credit him for starting me on my career path.

Thanks to my editor, Holly Davis of North Light Books, for her professional yet gentle expertise in completing this book, and to Kathy Kipp for tying up all the loose ends.

contents

materials

A good painting starts with good painting tools. The next few pages describe the paints, mediums, brushes and other materials I use and recommend. My materials list isn't long or complicated, but using these items can make all the difference in your painting. For help finding these materials, see "Where Can I Buy It" on page 11.

Robert Warren's Luminous Orange

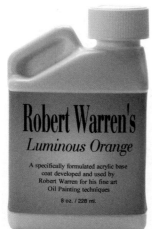

The goal of every painting is to capture light. I start almost all my oil paintings on an orange acrylic canvas. I came up with this idea about ten years ago after closely studying the work of Peter Paul Rubens—so closely in fact that I accidentally set off a museum alarm. I determined that Rubens' work had a certain luminous quality that many others from the same era did not. This luminosity seemed to come from within the painting rather than from the oil paint alone. I realized he had started his paintings on a toned canvas.

I experimented with different warm colors to act as my undertone. I started with a wash of burnt sienna, which proved to be too dark. Logically, I needed to go lighter—specifically to the color orange. As I continued to experiment, I realized that both the color intensity and the value of the orange were important factors. I was unable to find the exact color and value I needed among ready-made paints, so for quality control I started mixing my own. The specific color I came up with is now known as Luminous Orange.

I consider Luminous Orange to be the middle value of light. It serves as a wonderful value between highlights and shadows of any object. It offers "free" tints and shades of colors that can be subtle or rich. And it serves as a luminous reflected light in the shadows of many objects, from animals to landscapes to florals—basically anything that has light on it.

Following an important principle of design, the orange undertone adds a unity of color throughout the whole painting. The painting does not have to look obviously orange, but the color can peek through in every facet. Keep in mind as you paint that you're not trying to cover the orange canvas entirely; you're trying to capture the essence of light. You should be able to hold your completed painting in front of a light or window and see the orange glowing through the colors. For instructions on applying Luminous Orange, see page 12. If you prefer, you also can use a regular orange acrylic paint, but try to match its tone to mine as closely as possible.

Flat Black Acrylic

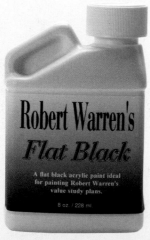

When painting with oils, placing dark and light pigments next to each other can be an accident waiting to happen. The term "mud" describes the outcome of trying to work with dark and light colors in close proximity. To end this problem, I've come up with a modern version of an Old Master's technique called grisaille, a term derived from the French word gris, meaning gray. This technique, dating back to the Gothic period and uses only gray oil paint tones, was originally used to give the illusion of sculpture or architecture. Later, painters glazed in thin layers over the gray tones as a means of saving their precious colored pigments. Today, paints are readily available, but my modern version of the grisaille value plan gives me a total understanding of the completed painting before adding the oil colors and makes creating mud virtually impossible.

Color usually receives all the attention, but it's values that create dimension My technique uses flat black acrylic paint instead of the oils as a value study. With the flat black, I establish the dark and middle values; the exposed orange canvas becomes the areas of lightest values. Again, this step gives a complete understanding of the textures and contrasts of the subject before the actual oil paint is applied. From details to large areas, values can be locked in place. Less oil paint is required, and the artist has more control throughout the painting.

Most flat black acrylic paint will work, but I have found some dry too quickly, such as black gessoes, while some decorative paints do not dry quickly enough. My Flat Black Acrylic is consistent and workable, yet it dries at a suitable rate. For flat black acrylic value painting techniques, see pages 13-17.

Robert Warren's Professional Clear Medium

Just before I begin painting with oils (generally after the value painting dries), I apply a clear medium to the entire canvas. This helps utilize both the light undertone of Luminous Orange and the dark and middle values of the black acrylic value study. The result is a painting full of rich, beautiful oil colors with luminous lights and invaluable dark values.

Every paint manufacturer has a clear glazing medium for oil paints that usually includes an oil with an alkyd drier added. Some speed up the drying process while some slow it down. Some smell so strong, they should only be used outdoors. Avoid any brands using linseed oil, which yellows.

After experimenting with many brands, I created my own Professional Clear Medium. It's an extremely effective, non-yellowing, odorless medium that creates a lubricated surface ideal for glazing oil paints. It also helps slow down brush wear. When applied, it's workable for two days and is mostly dry by the third day, depending on the humidity and temperatures. For instructions on applying this medium, see page 17

Oil Paint

Any oil paints will work with my techniques. Even with little experience, you will notice that the same color names may vary considerably between brands as well as the intensity or strength of colors. For all the projects in this book I used Martin/F. Weber products. My preferred white is Permalba White. For colors I use Prima Oil Colors. For more information about specific colors see page 21.

Brushes

The table below gives a complete listing of brushes I used for this book and describes the use for each type. A more specific brush list is given at the beginning of each project.

BRUSH NAME	SIZES	USE	PHOTO
FOAM	1-inch (25mm)	To apply Luminous Orange	
BRISTLE	1-inch (25mm)	To appy Professional Clear Medium	
SYNTHETIC FLAT	1/4-inch (6mm) & 1/2-inch (13mm)	For creating value paintings	
STIFF BRISTLE	No. 10	For thinner base colors of large areas	
BADGER FILBERT	Nos. 6 & 10	Used over base colors for painting the variable textures of nature	
HAKE	1-3/4 inch (44 mm)	For soft blending	
FAN	No. 4	Used only for Golden Ocean Sunset to create water movements	
LINE OR SCROLLER	No. 4	Used only for Back Harbor Morning as an optional choice for painting boat	

BRUSH CARE

To get the most out of your brushes, clean and store them properly after each use. Brush care isn't complicated, but the approach does depend on the brush type.

Foam Rather than clean out your foam brush after applying Luminous Orange, simply wrap it in plastic wrap to preserve it for your next application.

Synthetic Flats (acrylic brushes) Acrylic brushes, such as the synthetic flats used for value paintings, are cleaned with any type of mild soap (either bar or liquid) and water. I usually don't wash my brushes until I'm completely finished with the value painting, but if you do wash them before you finish, be sure to dry them thoroughly before adding more black acrylic paint.

1-inch (25mm) Bristle (for applying Professional Clear Medium) Clean this brush with odorless mineral spirits at the end of your painting session.

Oil Brushes Clean natural hair brushes between colors with baby oil. At the end of your painting session for the day, clean them with odorless mineral spirits in a well ventilated work space.

Other supplies

You'll need a few things besides paint, medium and brushes to round out your supplies. Save yourself some frustration by consulting the list below to make sure you have everything necessary.

Stretched Canvas Look for a bright white canvas with a medium texture—not too smooth, not too rough. Each project in this book is painted on a 12" × 16" (30cm × 41cm) canvas.

Pattern Painting patterns for all projects are provided on pages 121-126, but you'll need to enlarge them by the designated percentage with a photocopier.

Tracing paper Once your pattern is enlarged, you need to trace it onto this translucent paper.

Graphite paper This coated tissue-like paper allows you to transfer a pattern onto your canvas. I use either white or gray, depending on the undercoat.

Pen or pencil Used for tracing your pattern and transferring in onto your canvas. I recommend a red or blue ball point pen.

Small plastic container or cup For holding Luminous Orange and Professional Clear Medium.

Paper Towels Use a quality brand white paper towel to absorb excess medium (and to clean up messes).

Palette I prefer a disposable paper multi-palette made for both oils and acrylics.

Palette keeper This is an airtight container that holds a multi-palette pad. It allows you to keep your paints and mixtures fresh and safe for a few days, which really helps when you can't finish a project in one sitting. I recommend the Masterson Artist Palette Seal.

Palette knife Use this tool for mixing paint colors (see page 21). It can also be used for applying final shimmers or sparkles to water (see "Loading a Palette Knife," page 20).

Easel I recommend painting with your canvas on an easel, either free-standing or attached to a table. Be sure the easel is sturdy enough that the canvas stays attached when you press hard with your brush. Keeping your canvas at a comfortable face height allows you to step back to view and analyze your work.

Wipe out tool This tool has two different rubber tips from which to choose. It is used to remove paint for correcting or to wipe out desired effects in order to expose the Luminous Orange undertone.

Where can I buy it?

ROBERT WARREN'S LUMINOUS ORANGE, FLAT BLACK ACRYLIC AND PROFESSIONAL CLEAR MEDIUM	Send a written order or order through the Web: Robert Warren's Art Loft, 75 North High Street, Canal Winchester, Ohio 43110 www.robertwarrenartloft.com, Phone: 614.833.1033.
SCHARFF BRUSHES, MARTIN/F. WEBER PRIMA OIL COLORS, AND PERMALBA WHITE	Check your local art store or visit the Scharff Brushes, Inc. Web site: www.ArtBrush.com, and the Martin/F. Weber Web site: www.weberart.com
ADDITIONAL CONTACT INFORMATION FOR MARTIN/F. WEBER CO.:	(USA and International, except Canada) 2727 Southampton Road, Philadelphia, PA 19154-1293, Phone: 215.677.5600 (Canada) 26 Beaupre, Mercier, Quebec J6R 2J2, Phone: 866.484.4411
MASTERSON ARTIST PALETTE SEAL	Masterson Are Products Inc., P.O. Box 11301, Phoenix, AZ 85017 Phone: 800.965.2675, www.mastersonart.com
GENERAL PAINTING SUPPLIES	The materials mentioned on this and the previous pages are readily available at art and hobby stores. If you don't have these outlets nearby, enter the words "art supplies" into a Web search engine. The results will give you plenty of supply houses for ordering by mail or e-mail.

methods & techniques

Once you have all your materials collected, you'll probably want to jump right in with the painting. Hold off just a little longer to review the methods and practice the techniques presented on the next few pages. Your reward will be greater painting confidence and more satisfying results.

Canvas Preparation

Most of the paintings in this book start with an acrylic Luminous Orange undertone. Always apply this on a bright white canvas. An orange base over a gray or neutral canvas results in a dull or dirty orange with no luminous qualities. To best utilize the paint loaded on the foam brush, paint a few canvases instead of just one. Once the orange dries, transfer the pattern to your canvas.

1. Brush on Luminous Orange

Pour a little Luminous Orange into a small plastic cup. Use a 1-inch (25mm) foam brush to cover the canvas opaquely. Stroke both vertically and horizontally to get a nice smooth layer. Let dry.

2. Transfer the Pattern

Photocopy the appropriate pattern from the back of the book, enlarging it by the designated percentage to bring it to full size. Trace the pattern lines onto tracing paper. Place transfer paper, shiny side down, on the canvas and then the pattern over the transfer paper. Use a pen or pencil to trace over the pattern lines. The coating on the transfer paper will adhere to the canvas wherever you press, creating a reproduction of the pattern lines.

TRACING PATTERN LINES ON OILS

Occasionally you need to trace pattern lines over an area you've already painted with oils. In this case, no transfer paper is needed. Simply place your pattern over the painting and hold it lightly with one hand. Use a pencil or pen to trace the pattern lines into the wet paint. Remove the pattern. The pattern lines you just traced will show as orange lines.

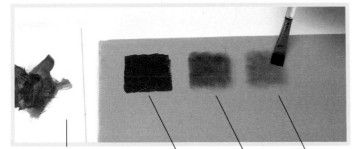

For drybrush values, wipe out the brush on the palette   dark value   medium value   light value

Black Values

All but two projects in this book utilize a flat black acrylic value painting. This gives you a complete understanding of your subject's textures and contrasts before the actual oil paint is applied. Use a ½-inch (13mm) or ¼-inch (6mm) synthetic flat, depending on the size of the area you're working on.

Use heavy, almost black paint for darkest values, a wiped-out brush or less paint for middle or gray values, and a very dry brush for the lightest value. I refer to the wiped-out brush as a drybrush. On a value scale from black to white, my focus is on the darkest and middle values.

Don't thin the paint with water. This will only flood the area with a dull gray tone, which defeats the purpose of the orange undertone. Drybrushing creates a "dot matrix" over the weave of the canvas by allowing some of the orange to show through. The small dots of black over the orange are extremely beneficial in accepting the glazes of oil color (see "Glazing" on page 20)

Value Painting Techniques

Following are different brushstroke techniques used for the value painting. Actually, these techniques can also be used with oils, but since they're crucial for the all-important value painting, they are being shown painted on Luminous Orange with black acrylic and a synthetic flat.

FIR OR PINE

1. Practice Making Triangles

Evergreen foliage is made up of different-sized triangles. To make these, hold the brush like a spoon, looking at the brush edge with the handle tilted about 45 degrees downward. Touch the corner to the canvas and press down without moving the brush. The harder you press, the larger the triangle. With the proper brush-handle angle, your triangles will have horizontal bottoms. Practice until you feel fairly competent.

2. Tap Trunk Line

Now begin the actual tree by using the edge of the brush to tap in a trunk line.

3. Tap in Texture

Build foliage texture with a series of overlapping triangles tapped from the top downward. Start with the smallest triangles at the top and increase the size as you move down the trunk (The triangles on the left show the scale of the triangles used to create the tree on the right.)

4. Completed Tree

Make both curved and angular branches of various lengths with the longer ones generally toward the tree bottom.

DECIDUOUS CLUMPS

1. Overview and Falling to the Right

Like fir and pine foliage, deciduous foliage clumps are formed by tapping in small-to-large triangular shapes, but the overall shape of the mass is different, depending on the distance or texture of the tree. In general, fill the clump center more solidly and create lacy or loose edges. Add variations to the way the clumps hang within a tree shape by letting the foliage fall to the right and the left. Lowering the angle of the brush handle makes the foliage fall to the right for right-handed painters and to the left for left-handed painters.

2. Falling to the Left

Raising the angle of the brush handle makes the foliage fall to the left for right-handed painters and to the right for left-handed painters.

3. Building Clumps in the Middle

For clumps in the middle of the tree, vary the angle of the handle so the overall effect doesn't lean too much to either the right or the left. Also note that an assortment of small, medium and large clumps create a tree.

SEPARATING FOLIAGE VALUES

As you view trees in nature, the foliage of one often overlaps that of another. Adjusting your values keeps the foliage from running together.

1. Paint First Tree with Diminishing Values

In this demonstration, the light is coming from the left. Fully load the brush and start tapping your foliage on the right, which is the most shaded area. As you continue to fill in the foliage toward the middle of the tree, the paint thins out, creating lighter values. Continue until you reach the left edge of the tree. The values will continue to diminish. Be sure to leave a few open sky holes.

2. Begin Second Tree with Darkest Values

Reload your brush before you start the second tree. Begin at the right edge of the second tree with your darkest values and work to the left as you did for the first tree. Notice that the contrast of darkest and lightest values separates the foliage of the two trees.

3. Go for Lacy Edges

Here you see a third tree added. When you start in with your darkest values, strive for a lacy effect on the edges. If a tree seems to be filling up with too much dark value, wipe out the brush a bit to lighten the value and continue.

PALMS

Palms appear only in one project in this book, "Tropical Surf & Shadows," and the technique for painting them is quite different from that of painting other trees.

1. Keep the Line Drawing Simplistic

Note that the line drawing shows just the centerline of the fronds.

2. Use Three Types of Strokes

For the trunk texture, achieve a wrap-around feeling by putting more pressure on one side of the brush.

Stroke the centerlines of the fronds with the chisel edge of the brush.

For the fronds, place the chisel edge of the brush on the canvas with one corner touching the centerline. Press slightly and then sweep down. Apply more pressure for a thicker frond.

ROCKS

Dark, medium and light values establish the planes and faces of rocks and give them dimension.

1. Establish Basic Shapes and Planes

Start with a line drawing. Notice that only a few planes are indicated.

2. Apply Darkest Values

Establish the darkest values first, which will be on the bottoms, between the rocks and on the shaded planes. Don't forget to ground the rocks with cast shadows. Note that as the paint dissipates, you'll get a bit of the middle value, which is desirable. Smallest rocks can be done impressionistically with a quick curved brushstroke, using the side of the brush.

3. Apply Middle Values

Add some lighter values on the partially shaded faces. Note that particularly on the larger rocks, the middle-value shading is stroked in a deliberate diagonal or sloping direction. Emphasize the planes' edges by accenting the dark planes where the lighter values meet the dark values, creating a sharp and definite ridge or shoulder.

4. Apply Lightest Gray Values

Add the lightest gray values. Leave some areas unpainted (orange) as highlight areas. Mountains are created in basically the same manner.

REFLECTIONS

In Still Water and Ice

To show reflections on still water or ice, just pull straight down on the flat of the brush.

In Water with Movement

To show water movement in your reflections, "squiggle" back and forth while pulling down on the flat of the brush. For firs, gradually tilt the brush to the corner to create a tapering shape. For rocks, make a more compressed squiggle.

Still Water Reflections

Reflections Showing Water Movement

Applying Professional Clear Medium

Professional Clear Medium is generally applied after the value painting is completed; however, two projects in this book do not utilize a black value painting. In these cases, the medium is applied immediately after pattern transfer. The method for applying the medium is the same whether you have a value painting or not, but without a value painting, you must take care not to lose your pattern lines.

1. Brush On the Medium

Shake the Professional Clear Medium well and squeeze about two teaspoons into a small plastic container. Use a 1-inch (25mm) bristle brush to apply the medium generously to the canvas. Use single-direction wet strokes. Avoid scrubbing, or you may lose your pattern lines. Go for a solid shine on the canvas.

2. Remove Excess Medium

Place one sheet of a quality brand paper towel on the canvas and stroke over it with the 1-inch (25mm) bristle brush. The excess medium will absorb into the towel. Reposition the towel until you have brushed over the entire canvas. You should have an even satin sheen with no heavy, wet areas. (Never rub the canvas with the paper towel—this creates an uneven coating.)

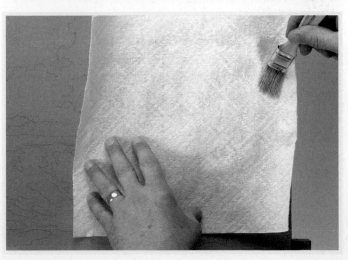

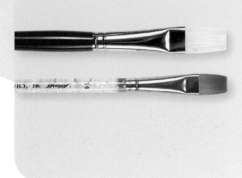

SYNTHETIC VS. NATURAL HAIR BRUSHES

The actual brushstroke techniques used in value paintings may be applied to both synthetic (for acrylics) and natural hair (for oils) brushes, but brushes made from natural hair or bristles swell and change their shape when used with a water-based paint. Acrylic paint is water-based, so it must be used with a synthetic brush, which will retain its shape. The acrylic paint establishes very important values, but the brushstrokes don't need to have the finesse of the oil detail.

Oil Strokes & Techniques

Once you apply the clear medium, you're ready to add color with oils. These paints have their own set of strokes and techniques, which are easily mastered.

FOLIAGE STROKE

The foliage strokes for oils is basically the same as for acrylics, except you use a natural-hair filbert and hold the brush as you would a pencil.

Deciduous

Note how deciduous foliage shapes and clumps are created with the positioning of color and values. The midvalue helps establish the clumps. The highlight is applied toward the tops of the clumps.

Fir or Pine

With firs and pines, you use the midvalue to establish the branches. The highlight is applied sparingly on the tops of the branches. Apply the paint with overlapping downward touches, using the tip of the brush.

BLOTTING STROKE

The blotting stroke is used for adding color in nondescript shapes, such as the deciduous foliage to the right. Apply by pressing down repeatedly with the flat broadside of the brush. At the top of the photo you see the stroke by itself. Below this you see the stroke being applied to foliage.

Deciduous Foliage Stroke

Fir and Pine Foliage Stroke

Blotting stroke by itself

Blotting stroke applied to foliage to add green color in dark areas.

Blotting Stroke

ROCK HIGHLIGHTING

Highlighting on rock generally establishes the top face, which receives most of the light. The same technique is used to establish the tops of mounds or the terrain of snowbanks.

1. Stroke on the Color

Stroke color across the top of the highlight area for definition.

2. Blend

Stroke the bottom edge of the highlight stroke, blending it into the slope of the rock shape.

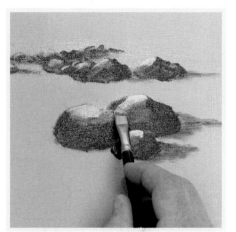 

BROAD STROKE & EDGE STROKE

For a broad stroke, pull down on the full width of the brush. For an edge stroke, pull on the edge of the brush.

Horizontal & Vertical Strokes

Sometimes the project instructions refer to horizontal and vertical strokes. These are nothing more than broad strokes (vertical) and edge strokes (horizontal). They're used for reflections in water or to fill in a nondescript shape.

Mopping with a Hake Brush

Mopping or blending with a hake brush eliminates brushstrokes. It may be done in the middle of a project and is always done as a finishing touch. Simply brush gently across the indicated areas.

Broad Stroke

Edge Stroke

Horizontal and Vertical Strokes

Mopping with a Hake Brush

SCOOP BRUSH LOAD

A brush loaded with the scoop technique creates more definition or sharpness, particularly when used to add final highlights.

1. Slide into the Paint

Slide the brush edge into the paint. Note the small paint bead forming at the brush tip.

2. Note the bead

This is what the loaded brush looks like.

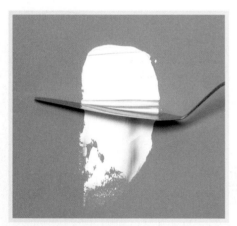

LOADING A PALETTE KNIFE

A palette knife works well for applying final shimmers or sparkles to water because the knife doesn't overblend the sharp lines as a brush does.

1. Flatten & Slide

Flatten the paint. Then slide the knife through the paint at a slight angle.

2. Loaded Knife

The paint loads on the bottom of the knife.

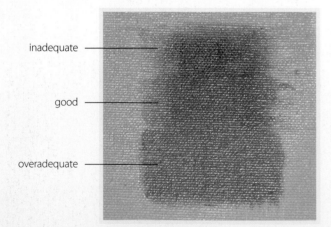

inadequate

good

overadequate

Glazing Thicknesses

GLAZING

A reminder that a glaze results from pigmented color that becomes more transparent when applied or worked into the Professional Clear Medium. The goal of glazing is to add color while still utilizing the undertones of the orange base color and the black value painting.

As in all but two of the projects in this book, a semi-transparent glaze would be applied over the black to gray value painting done on a Luminous Orange based canvas. The photo on the left shows a progression of glazing thickness from which to compare. Typically, a glaze is the first color thinly applied to most areas and objects. When done to the right thickness, it allows progressively thicker amounts of middle values and highlights to be applied without too much paint buildup. A good glaze applies just enough paint to smooth out the grainy black acrylic middle value texture on the canvas. An inadequate glaze lets the black value painting show through too much. An over heavy glaze covers the orange and black too much, losing the undertones.

Straight Colors

Here you see samples of all the straight oil colors I use in the projects. I recommend Martin/F. Weber oils, but you may match colors from other brands if you prefer.

PERMALBA WHITE **CADMIUM YELLOW LIGHT** **CADMIUM YELLOW MEDIUM** **NAPLES YELLOW**

PEACH **TURQUOISE** **PHTHALO GREEN** **SAP GREEN**

PRIMA PINK **CADMIUM RED LIGHT** **COBALT BLUE** **COBALT VIOLET** **ALIZARIN CRIMSON** **CADMIUM RED MEDIUM**

RAW SIENNA **IVORY BLACK** **PRIMA GRAY** **BURNT UMBER** **BURNT SIENNA**

Mixtures

You'll use the colors listed above far more as components of mixtures than as the straight colors. There are two methods for mixing colors, depending on the amount of the mixture you need.

Measured Mixture

At the beginning of each project, you'll find a list of straight colors and the quantity of that color used. This quantity is measured as the length of the paint bead as it comes out of the tube (1/2" [13mm], 1/4" [6mm], 1/8" [3mm], a touch).

Each project also gives formulas for its paint mixtures. To make a mixture, use a palette knife to slice the correct portions from the straight colors you've already measured out. Then combine all the mixture colors in the formula with a palette knife.

The same straight color name will probably vary in color and intensity from brand to brand. Any brand will work, but you may have to adjust the amounts. Also consider the different sizes of tube openings among brands.

Brush Mixtures

For mixtures in small quantities, simply use your brush to pull the colors out of the paint pile and mix. Formulas for brush mixtures appear parenthetically within the step-by-step instructions.

Measured Mixture

Brush Mixture

Golden Ocean Sunset

LIFE DOESN'T GET MUCH BETTER than painting with friends, enjoying good food and music and gathering on the white-sand beach to enjoy one of nature's best shows—the sunset. That's what happens yearly during my workshop in Cozumel, Mexico. Sunsets are beautiful anywhere, but they seem even more spectacular when your toes are buried in the sand and you're looking out over the ocean.

In this painting, the contrasting dark clouds and their reflections hold their place with the black acrylic undertones while the Luminous Orange canvas helps illuminate the warm reds, oranges and golds. Your challenge is not to blend the cool blues and purples too much into the opposite warm colors of the golden light.

materials

SURFACE
Stretched Canvas, 12" × 16"
   (30cm × 41cm)

ACRYLIC
Luminous Orange

Flat Black

OIL
Martin/F. Weber Permalba White
   - 2" (51mm)

Martin/F. Weber Prima Oil Color
   Cadmium Yellow Medium
     - ¼" (6mm)

   Cadmium Red Light - ½" (13mm)

   Cobalt Violet - ½" (13mm)

   Ivory Black - ¼" (6mm)

   Cobalt Blue - ¼" (6mm)

   Naples Yellow - ⅛" (3mm)

   Turquoise - ⅛" (3mm)

   Cadmium Yellow Light
     - ⅛" (3mm)

BRUSHES
Foam, 1-inch (25mm)
   (to apply Luminous Orange)

Bristle, 1-inch (25mm)
   (to apply medium)

Synthetic flat, ½-inch (13mm)

Badger filbert, no. 10

Hake, 1¾-inch (44mm)

Fan, no. 4

OTHER MATERIALS
Robert Warren's Professional
   Clear Medium

Palette knife (for mixing paint)

Wipe out tool

Pattern (see page 121)

Dark   Dark   Dark   Dark   Dark

1. Value Painting (½-inch [13mm] synthetic flat)

Prepare the canvas for the value painting as described on page 12. Use flat black acrylic for the value painting (see pages 13-17 for value-painting techniques).

Define the horizon line. Then create gray tones, stroking lower into the water by using less paint and a drier brush. Using the edge of your brush and horizontally stroking side to side, paint dark cloud reflections in the water, creating black to gray values. Add a few very low wave lines, even through the light areas across the canvas. Use the corner or side of the brush to scrub in cloud top shapes. Stretch out or taper both large and thin cloud bottoms, using a horizontal scrub with the brush edge. Don't fill in the clouds too solidly.

Allow the black acrylic value painting to dry. Apply Professional Clear Medium as described on page 17.

GOLD
¼" (6mm) each of White & Cadmium Yellow Medium

RED-ORANGE
¼" (6mm) Cadmium Red Light + ⅛" (3mm) White

PLUM
⅛" (3mm) each of Cobalt Violet & Cadmium Red Light + a touch of Ivory Black

PALE BLUE-GRAY
¼" (6mm) White + a touch each of Cobalt Blue & Cobalt Violet & Naples Yellow

2. Lower Sky & Reflections (No. 10 badger filbert)

Paint **Gold** around the sun, stretching the color left and right. Also work it between the cloud shapes above the sun. Start the sun reflection by adding a vertical streak the width of the sun from the horizon to the bottom of the canvas. Paint **Red-Orange** low on the sky horizon, stretching it into the gold. Glaze over the low, flat cloud shapes, the large sky shapes above the sun and the bottoms of all the upper clouds. Add cloud reflections with vertical strokes glazed into the light areas of the water. Apply more color, extending about two inches (51mm) from each side of the sun reflection streak.

Sun

3. Lower Sky & Reflections (No. 10 badger filbert)

Add vertical **Gold** streaks in the water by sweeping downward and tapering off into the Red-Orange reflections at the bottom of the canvas. These streaks are brightest around the sun reflections. Glaze **Plum** over the sky horizon, working from the sides of the canvas toward the sun. Carefully add a layer of glaze on the underside of the low clouds. Glaze over the middle areas of the upper clouds, extending outward into the Red-Orange profile color. Glaze horizontally over the water horizon, stroking from the sides of the canvas toward the sun. Stroke the glaze on the dark reflections from the horizon downward and from the bottom of the canvas upward, blending into the Red-Orange.

LIGHT BLUE
¼" (6mm) White + a touch each of Cobalt Blue & Cobalt Violet

DARK BLUE-GRAY
¼" (6mm) White + ⅛" (3mm) each of Cobalt Blue & Cobalt Violet & Ivory Black

LIGHT TURQUOISE
¼" (6mm) White + ⅛" (3mm) Turquoise

4. Open Sky (No. 10 badger filbert)

Paint the lower open sky area with **Pale Blue-Gray,** working loosely around the cloud shapes with many interlocking negative shapes into the clouds (see sidebar below). Blend into the lower Gold for a very slight greenish tint. Paint upper open sky with **Light Blue,** working into the edges and around the clouds. Add Medium Blue (brush mix Light Blue mix + a touch each of Cobalt Blue & Cobalt Violet) to the top of the sky, blending into the Light Blue.

5. Open Sky (No. 10 badger filbert)

Loosely blot and stroke **Dark Blue-Gray** into the middles of the cloud shapes and work it in and out of the edges, picking up a little open sky color and softening some of the profile edges. Create formations inside the clouds. Add some of this color into the low cloud streaks and the horizon water. Avoid the glow under the sun.

INTERLOCKING SHAPES

Cloud shapes as well as deciduous tree shapes should interlock with their negative spaces or the sky. Analyze not only the shape of the object, but also the negative space around the object. Clouds and deciduous trees have similar interlocking type shapes and spaces around them. If the sky area could be pulled out of a cloud shape smoothly, it is not an interlocking shape, not realistic and could take on a cartoon-like appearance. Learning to look for interlocking shapes and adding these characteristics to your paintings will create more natural and spontaneous artwork.

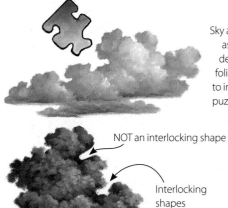

Sky and clouds as well as deciduous foliage need to interlock as puzzle pieces.

NOT an interlocking shape

Interlocking shapes

6. Water Movements (No. 4 fan)

Load **Dark Blue-Gray** on one side of the no. 4 fan brush and drag with a light touch in horizontal thin strokes to create distant water movements. Do the same with wider strokes to create close water movements. Taper these surface movement streaks as your drag them toward the sun reflection. Let a few streaks cross through the sun reflection.

7. Clouds & Water (No. 10 badger filbert & no. 4 fan)

Returning to the no. 10 badger filbert, add a few **Light Turquoise** reflected light highlights to the shaded formations inside the clouds. Then load the fan brush and drag this reflected light into the Dark Blue-Gray streaks in the water.

8. Water Highlights (No. 10 badger filbert)

Scoop **Light Turquoise** on the chisel edge of the no. 10 badger filbert to create the "cupped" highlights in the closest water. Use a very light touch, and hold the brush perpendicular to the canvas. *Tip:* Keep the natural perspective in mind for adding the shimmers or highlights to water. Distant movements are compressed together and separate when coming close.

9. Sun Glow & Reflections (No. 10 badger filbert)

Paint the bottom, flat area of the sun "ball" with **Cadmium Yellow Light**. Add a few edge strokes in the thin gold areas around the sun and add horizontal edge strokes to the vertical sun streak shimmers in the water. Add **White** to the Cadmium Yellow Light for a very light-yellow brush mix. Accent the bottom edges of the closest clouds around the sun. Apply a bit of this color to the ball-like top of the sun. Add horizontal accent shimmers to the sun reflection in the water. Then use an extremely light touch to add a vertical streak in the open sky above the dark cloud over the sun. Blend this into the open sky.

10. Sun, Water & Cloud Details (No. 10 badger filbert)

Accent the roundness of the sun with **White.** Add a few white highlight accents to the water shimmers in the sun's reflection. Use **Ivory Black** to add a darker value to each side (above and below) of the water horizon line. Suggest and blend a few dark accents on the bottoms of the largest middle and upper clouds. Then use a wipe out tool to pick off a few bottom edges of the upper clouds. This exposes a bit of the orange acrylic, creating a backlighting effect.

GOLDEN OCEAN SUNSET

Finishing Touches (Hake)

Mop the edges and middle areas of the clouds. Also mop to stretch out the sun glow spaces and cloud edges horizontally. Finish by mopping the water horizontally. Be sure to wipe off the brush between strokes. (See page 19 for an explanation of mopping.)

Autumn Lake

I'VE BEEN VERY FORTUNATE in my workshop travels to discover many beautiful parts of the United States, particularly on the northeast and northwest coasts. Both areas are home to many picturesque watery coves and inlets like the one you see in this painting.

Although a simple scene, this painting offers many valuable techniques. In the black acrylic value study, I created a focal point of a high contrast area of light autumn foliage against the very dark fir trees. This painting also features high impact color contrast with the bright blue lower sky complimenting the orange and gold deciduous trees. The cold, clear water reflections are accented by using a slightly darker value of their counterparts.

materials

SURFACE

Stretched Canvas, 12" × 16"
(30cm × 41cm)

ACRYLIC

Luminous Orange

Flat Black

OIL

Martin/F. Weber Permalba White
1½" (38mm)

Martin/F. Weber Prima Oil Colors
Turquoise - ¼" (6mm)
Cobalt Blue - ½" (13mm)
Cobalt Violet - ½" (13mm)
Ivory Black - ½" (13mm)
Burnt Umber - ¼" (6mm)
Sap Green - ¼" (6mm)
Raw Sienna - ⅛" (3mm)
Burnt Sienna - ⅛" (3mm)
Naples Yellow - ⅛" (3mm)

BRUSHES

Foam, 1-inch (25mm) (to apply
Luminous Orange)

Bristle, 1-inch (25mm)
(to apply medium)

Synthetic flat, ¼-inch (6mm)

Stiff bristle, no 10

Badger filbert, no.10

Hake, 1¾-inch (44mm)

OTHER MATERIALS

Robert Warren's Professional
Clear Medium

Palette knife (for mixing paint and
adding water shimmers)

Pattern (see page 121)

1. Value Painting (¼-inch [6mm] synthetic flat)

Prepare the canvas for the value painting as described on page 12. Use flat black acrylic for the value painting (see pages 13-17 for value-painting techniques).

Starting on the left, define the darkest background trees down to the top profiles of the deciduous trees. Loosely outline the shoreline. Create rock impressions on distant peninsulas. Add contours to baselines for tree-line foliage. Show dark profiles above the rocks and the shadows between rocks. Add a few squiggly tree reflections in the bottom left corner and middle section of the lake.

Allow the black acrylic value painting to dry. Apply Professional Clear Medium as described on page 17.

2. Sky & Water (No. 10 stiff bristle brush)

Use **Light Turquoise** (brush mix equal amounts of White + Turquoise) to fill in the bottom half of the sky area, working around the clouds and into the areas between trees. Add a little more Turquoise to create a darker value for the water. Sweep over the reflections, using vertical broad strokes and horizontal edge strokes. Work the mixture between the reflections.

3. Sky & Water (No. 10 stiff bristle brush)

Fill in the remaining sky area with **Blue-Gray**. Do the same in the water area, filling in the bottom of the canvas, but avoiding the cloud reflection area. Work around reflections, using vertical broad strokes and horizontal edge strokes. Blend in more **Light Turquoise** if the color gets too dark. Thinly glaze over the dark tree reflections, sweeping into the water, still using vertical broad strokes and horizontal edge strokes.

4. Clouds & Cloud Reflections (No. 10 badger filbert)

Using blotting, circular strokes, fill in the cloud areas and their corresponding water reflections with **White**. Add a speck of **Turquoise** to the brush to create a darker value for edges of the cloud reflections. With a wiped-out brush, distort the reflections by sweeping vertically over the reflections, using vertical broad strokes and horizontal zigzag strokes in and out of the cloud edges.

5. Distant Hills & Their Reflections (No. 10 badger filbert)

Glaze **Purple Gray** over the distant hills and their water reflections, using contouring strokes to suggest the hillside slopes. *Note:* Reflections are always darker than the actual object they're reflecting. That's why in step 2 you add Turquoise to the mix for the sky reflection.

BLUE-GRAY
⅛" (3mm) each of White & Cobalt Blue & Cobalt Violet + ¼" (6mm) Ivory Black

PURPLE-GRAY
⅛" (3mm) White + ¼" (6mm) Cobalt Violet + ⅛" (3mm) Ivory Black

DARK GREEN
¼" (6mm) each of Cobalt Blue & Burnt Umber

GRAY-GREEN
¼" (6mm) White + ⅛" (3mm) each of Dark Green Mix & Sap Green

6. Distant Firs (No. 10 badger filbert)

Tap in the most distant, lighter-value fir tree impressions with **Purple/Blue-Gray** (brush mix equal amounts of Blue-Gray + Purple-Gray). Overwork into the sky color to soften the trees, creating a distant effect.

7. Firs, Deciduous Trees & Their Reflections (No. 10 badger filbert)

Restate the darkest values on the fir trees with **Dark Green**, maintaining the delicate treetops. Also work this color into the negative shapes of the lower foliage. Allow very small gaps of orange background to show through. Glaze over the lower darkness of the deciduous trees. Sweep vertically over the dark reflections, using broad strokes. Add horizontal zigzag strokes. Don't forget the cove area reflections.

8. Water Shimmers (Palette knife & optional no. 10 badger filbert)

Load **White** on the edge of a palette knife and skip and drag across the horizon line (see "Loading a Palette Knife" on page 20). Add horizontal water shimmers with light edge touches. Make sure you add a couple of shimmer dashes between the firs. The most distant shimmer on the horizon should be more solid (you may need to use no. 10 badger filbert brush for this). *Tip:* Using the palette knife for shimmers keeps the paint from blending and creates a more shimmering effect.

9. Water Shimmers (Hake)

Carefully mop horizontally across the water shimmers with the hake brush.

10. Trees & Banks (No. 10 badger filbert)

Use **Dark Green** to restate the two right dark trees and the rocky shore point. Make this point overlap the distant water. With **Blue-Gray**, glaze over the dark edge of the middle distant bank and the shaded rocks on the closest bank edge and on the shaded area under the left trees.

11. Rocks (No. 10 badger filbert)

Use **Purple Gray** to accent the rock tops and to suggest their top profiles in the shadows, creating small, medium, and large sizes.

12. Firs, Low Foliage & Water Reflections (No. 10 badger filbert)

Use **Gray Green** to add middle values to the fir trees and to the distant low foliage on the rocky shore point. Add a few vertical and horizontal reflections to the water, corresponding to the fir trees.

13. Autumn Foliage & Water Reflections
(No. 10 badger filbert)

Blot **Raw Sienna** into the light tops of the deciduous trees and glaze the wedge of light on the slope of the bank. Tap **Burnt Sienna** texture into the lower foliage of the deciduous trees. With the same color, add vertical strokes to the dark water reflections.

14. Autumn Foliage & Slope
(No. 10 badger filbert)

Scoop Naples Yellow onto the brush tip and add lacy edges to the tops and the middle areas of the deciduous trees. Accent the top slope of the shore area by these trees and blend.

15. Trunks, Branches & Accent Highlights
(No. 10 badger filbert)

Suggest tree trunks and branches in deciduous trees with **Dark Green**. With **Yellow-Green** (brush mix Sap Green + White), lightly sprinkle a highlight accent on the fir trees and the bushes on the bank. Do not highlight all the firs, only those in the focal point area of the autumn color foliage.

16. Deciduous Tree Reflections
(No. 10 badger filbert)

Very sparingly, suggest vertical and horizontal touches of **Raw Sienna** to the water reflections in the cove and on the left, corresponding to the deciduous trees.

17. Rock Faces & Water Movement (No. 10 badger filbert)

Use **Light Lavender Gray** (brush mix White + a touch of Purple-Gray) to selectively highlight rock faces, paying special attention to the area of the painting where the sunlight is hitting. Create small, medium and large rocks. Add a hint (but don't outline) of water movement on edge of the upper and lower banks. If you've made too many highlights, go over rocks with **Dark Green**. Leave an empty area with no detail on the far left. If necessary, restate the dark shadows between the rocks lining the bank edges.

17

AUTUMN LAKE

Finishing Touches (Hake)

With a hake brush, mop the water horizontally. Be sure to wipe the brush on a paper towel between strokes. (See page 19 for an explanation of mopping.)

Tropical Surf & Shadows

 **I'M THANKFUL FOR THE OPPORTUNITIES** I've had to vacation and teach in Cozumel, Mexico with many of my more enthusiastic and fun-loving students and friends. These trips have been a Caribbean fantasy for painters, photographers and snorkelers. The flora, fauna and beautiful turquoise water offer endless painting ideas, and the ambiance of warm, shallow waters with shimmering light patterns and tropical shadows on white sands lifts both emotions and creativity to a higher level.

In this painting you'll capture some of the above-mentioned essences with the use of warm lights and cool shadows, even underwater. You'll also learn a great technique for transferring pattern lines on a wet canvas.

materials

1. Value Painting (¼-inch [6mm] synthetic flat)

Prepare the canvas for the value painting as described on page 12. Use flat black acrylic for the value painting (see pages 13-17 for value-painting techniques).

Base in the palm fronds with the flat edge of brush. Using broad, flat, curved strokes, define the tree trunk. Holding the brush horizontally, create palm shadows in the water and soften their edges with a drier brush. Outline the rock bases and add dimension. Lightly outline the shoreline and the under-breaking waves. Drag gray value across the horizon line and add the shallow water lines left from previous waves. Scrub shadows between the rocks and add shadows to the sand area.

Allow the black acrylic value painting to dry. Apply Professional Clear Medium as described on page 17.

LAVENDER-BLUE	LIGHT BLUE	CREAM	DARK GREEN	BLUE GREEN
⅛" (3mm) Cobalt Blue + ¼" (6mm) Cobalt Violet + ½" (13mm) White	½" (13mm) White + a touch of Cobalt Blue	¼" (6mm) White + a touch of Naples Yellow	¼" (6mm) each of Cobalt Blue & Burnt Umber	⅛" (3mm) each of Dark Green mix & White & Turquoise

Foam & Light Overlay

Use this overlay for step 15 to trace the foam patterns. Enlarge at 200 percent, then enlarge at 200 percent to bring up to full size. This overlay may be hand-traced or photocopied for personal use only.

2. Sky (No. 10 stiff bristle brush)

Paint **Lavender-Blue** halfway down the sky area, going around—but not fully avoiding—the palm fronds. Make sure to go slightly into the fronds in order not to create a halo effect. Paint in the remaining sky with **Light Blue**, using the corner of the brush to go around the clouds. Blend and blot into the **Lavender-Blue**. Add **White** to the **Light Blue** and paint the stripe of most distant sky down to the water.

3. Clouds (No. 10 badger filbert)

Use **Cream** to blot in the tops, left sides and middles of the clouds shapes, allowing some orange to show through. Consider that the shadows will be on the right sides and bottoms.

LAVENDER
¼" (6mm) White + ⅛" (3mm) Cobalt Violet + a touch of Cobalt Blue

PALE LAVENDER
¼" (6mm) White + a touch of Lavender mix

4. Clouds (No. 10 badger filbert)

Blot and stroke **Lavender-Blue** into the shaded areas of the clouds, working into the Cream to create a lighter value. Use the Lavender-Blue to define the cloud bottoms and to stretch out a few clouds in the horizon. Add light touches of **Light Blue** in the middles of the clouds, between the shadows and highlights. *Tip:* For natural perspective in clouds, the bottoms always flatten closer to the horizon.

5. Horizon & Water (No. 10 badger filbert)

Use **Lavender-Blue** to define the horizon, continuing down about ½-inch (13mm) into the water to the top of the far wave crest (see parts of a wave on page 58).

6. Water (No. 10 badger filbert)

Glaze in **Blue-Green**, slightly overlapping the **Lavender-Blue**. Use sweeping horizontal strokes. Then base in the crest of the closer wave, blending downward into the black acrylic horizontal surf lines and sweeping upward into the windows of the wave above.

7. Water (No. 10 badger filbert)

Use **Dark Green** to restate the darkest values at the base of the waves, working the color into the **Blue-Green** glaze.

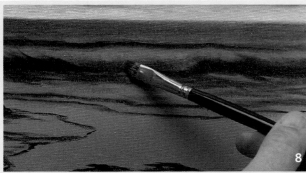

8. Breaking Foam (No. 10 badger filbert)

Add **Lavender-Blue** to the bottom of the breaking foam.

9. Water (No. 10 badger filbert)

Using the edge of the brush, add a few **Light Blue** crests to the most distant water. Also add a defining line to the crest of the further wave. Add a few horizontal blue lines in the small space between the two waves (trough area). Place this blue at the top of the near wave on either side of the crashing foam. Scoop Light Blue onto the brush tip and place horizontal movements in front of the closest wave, sweeping upward into the contour of closest wave. Add more Light Blue on top of the dark surf lines. Finally, fill in the closer, shallow water down to the palm shadow.

10. Water (No. 10 badger filbert)

Apply **Lavender** from the bottom of the canvas up into the Light Blue water, blending where the colors meet. Use horizontal scrubbing strokes. Butt the color up against the rocks, rock shadows and palm shadows, letting orange show through slightly. With **Dark Lavender-Blue** (brush mix Lavender-Blue + Cobalt Blue), glaze over the palm shadows with horizontal strokes, blending slightly into the Lavender.

11. Sandbar & Rocks (No. 10 badger filbert)

Using **Brown** (brush mix Prima Gray + Burnt Umber), horizontally glaze over the sandbar, working around the rocks. Glaze **Burnt Umber** over all the rocks, using directional strokes. Work the color into the sand to create shadows around the rock bottoms.

12. Rocks & Sandbar (No. 10 badger filbert)

Add middle values on the rocks with **Prima Gray**, emphasizing the rock slopes with chisel-edge strokes. Highlight the rocks with **Peach** on the left and top slopes. Also highlight the sand, working horizontally around the shadows. Blend the peach into the shadows and add a few mounds to the sand.

13. Rocks & Sandbar (No. 10 badger filbert)

Use **Cream** to accent the rock tops and the left slopes. Also use this color to define the sand at the water edge and to highlight the sand surface. Avoid filling in with this color too solidly. Add just a few strokes of **Light Blue** to show sky reflections on the shaded sides of the rocks.

14. Water (No. 10 badger filbert)

Lightly drag **Pale Lavender** across the horizon and distant water to create shimmers. Using the brush edge, apply this color to the tops of the waves. Add a few horizontal edge strokes to the wave troughs (areas between crests) and to the water in front of the closest wave. Scoop paint on the brush tip and add it to the top edges of the close surf lines. Still using scooped paint, apply this color around the sandbar, zigzagging into the sand.

15. Light Patterns in Water (No. 10 badger filbert)

Place the Foam & Light overlay (see page 41) on the wet painting and press in the water line patterns with a pen or pencil (see "Tracing Pattern Lines on Oils," page 12).

16. Light Patterns in Water (No. 10 badger filbert)

Using the chisel edge or brush tip, follow the orange pattern lines to create **Pale Lavender** light patterns in the water. Allow the blue in the shadows to blend into the Pale Lavender, which will create a darker value. If the water lines get too blended, add more paint and rehighlight select areas, staying out of the shadows. If the lines seem too thick, use **Lavender** to brush blend some of them out. If you lose palm shadows, bring them back with a brush mix of **Lavender-Blue + Dark Green.**

17. Water (No. 10 badger filbert)

Add **Cream** to the crest of the breaking waves. Also stretch the color out thinly on the edge of the sand, into the surf lines and into a few of the water pattern lines (but not across the palm shadows).

18. Palm Trunk (No. 10 badger filbert)

Lightly glaze **Prima Gray** over the entire tree trunk. Add **Peach** to highlighted areas.

19. Palm Trunk (No. 10 badger filbert)

Add an accent highlight of **Pale Lavender** to the trunk. Restate the trunk texture with **Dark Green**, wrapping the color around the trunk.

20. Fronds (No. 10 badger filbert)

Still using the **Dark Green**, define the centerlines of the fronds and restate the frond leaves with the chisel edge of the brush. Reload brush with fresh paint as necessary. Blot in the middle area where the fronds come together to create a solid mass. Allow some orange background to show slightly between the frond leaves, but glaze over if too much is showing. Accent the dark areas of the rocks if necessary.

21. Fronds, Trunk & Rocks (No. 10 badger filbert)

Highlight the fronds with **Yellow-Green** (brush mix equal touches of Sap Green + White). Add **Naples Yellow** accent highlights to the fronds and in touches to the underside of the tree trunk as a reflected light. Then add **Lavender-Blue** reflected light in the shadow areas on the top of the trunk and shaded right side of rocks.

TROPICAL SURF & SHADOWS

Finishing Touches (Hake)

Horizontally mop the distant and close water and clouds. Carefully avoid mopping the palm fronds and rocks. (See page 19 for an explanation of mopping.)

Water Lily Pond

I'VE TRAVELED ALL OVER THE WORLD taking reference photos, but sometimes I find something magical in my own backyard. This lily pond is a perfect example.

Don't let the simplicity of the subject fool you. This painting employs unique techniques that have to be handled appropriately. The brush techniques used in the upper background offer an impressionistic interpretation but are actually realistic distortions of the sky and tree reflections as they transition into the dark underwater rocks of the foreground.

The colorful overlapping lily pads are unified with the sky color and "stitched" onto the water surface with tiny sparkling highlights. The delicate colors of the sunlit blossoms with their shadows form a dimensional focal point, while the varied sizes help create perspective.

materials

1. Value Painting (½-inch [13mm] synthetic flat)

Prepare the canvas for the value painting as described on page 12. Use flat black acrylic for the value painting (see pages 13-17 for value-painting techniques).

   Paint around the lily pads and cover the upper background almost entirely black. On the bottom third of the canvas, use a drier brush to apply a few bumps of gray with some orange background showing through (these will later suggest underwater rocks). Wipe out the brush and add gray tones in a spoke-like application to all the pads. Outline all the lily pad edges that overlap each other. Allow the black acrylic value painting to dry. Apply Professional Clear Medium as described on page 17.

2. Background Water (No. 10 stiff bristle brush)

Using very little **Dark Blue** and broad vertical and horizontal strokes, work from the top of the canvas down into the lily pads, diminishing into the bottom area. Avoid the light reflection area in the top middle part of the canvas. Touch the background color to some of the lily pad edges to avoid "haloes" (the obvious characteristic of working around an object and leaving an empty space).

3. Light Area in Water
(No. 10 stiff bristle brush)

Establish the light area at the top and middle of the canvas using **Lavender-Blue** and short vertical and horizontal strokes.

4. Light Area in Water
(No. 10 stiff bristle brush)

Repeat the last step with **Turquoise**, taking care not to blend too much. Add **White** to the brush for a lighter value and re-accent. Use **Light Yellow** (brush mix Naples Yellow + White) to accent the brightest middle area.

DARK BLUE
¼" (6mm) Cobalt Violet +⅛" (3mm) each of Cobalt Blue & White

LAVENDER-BLUE
½" (13mm) White + ⅛" (3mm) each of Cobalt Blue & Cobalt Violet

DARK GREEN
¼" (6mm) each of Sap Green & Burnt Umber & Cobalt Blue

PURPLE
¼" (6mm) Cobalt Violet + a touch of Cobalt Blue

YELLOW-GREEN
¼" (6mm) each of Sap Green & White

5. Rocks
(No. 10 stiff bristle brush & hake)

Using **Burnt Sienna**, create underwater impressions of the rocks in the lower portion of the canvas. Work between the lily pads, occasionally touching their edges to avoid haloes. Add touches of **Lavender-Blue** to the brush for a few dull, blurred rock highlights. With **Burnt Umber**, darken any areas as necessary. Use light horizontal and vertical strokes to mop the painting with a hake brush.

6. Lily Pads (No. 10 stiff bristle brush)

Glaze **Dark Green** very thinly over the flat lily pads, using spoke-like strokes from the outer edges toward the middle. Use just enough paint to give the black-to-gray acrylic values of the lily pads a blended or smooth appearance.

Tip: The lily pads have more than six colors. Be very minimal with the amount of paint in each step. Remember, you can always go back and add more paint later.

Cupped Pad

Cupped Pad

7. Lily Pads (No. 10 badger filbert)

With **Purple**, apply spoke-like strokes on the inside of the two smaller, cupped lily pads. Also add a few strokes to the larger lily pads. Use this color to place cast shadows under the four flower petals over the pads. Apply **Dark Red** (brush mix Purple mix + Alizarin Crimson) to the undersides of the cupped pads. Add a few strokes into the flat pads.

8. Lily Pads (No. 10 badger filbert)

Add a midvalue of **Yellow-Green** to the flat lily pads by laying the side of the brush on the edge of the pad and sweeping inward. This creates clean outer edges. Use less paint and a lighter stroke on the smaller pads. Add **Light Turquoise** (brush mix Turquoise + White) accents to all flat pads, sometimes stroking from the outer edges to the middle and sometimes vice versa. Accent the brightest lights on all pads with **Naples Yellow**. Emphasize the light around the petal shadows and use a spoke-like direction for your strokes. Frequently wipe off the brush with a paper towel and replenish with clean color.

9. Lily Pads (No. 10 badger filbert)

Restate the dark values on the flat pads with **Dark Blue**. Also add this color to the inside of the cupped pads. Pull strokes from the inside out. Add a few **Lavender-Blue** accents to the darker areas of all the pads.

10. Lily Pads (No. 10 badger filbert)

Add tiny dashes of **White** light under the edges of a few pads. Use an extremely light touch with the very edge of the brush. Also add a White accent on the closer pads around the two blossom shadows.

Tip: For any subject, a good rule to remember is to never let a highlight reach the edge of the canvas. This will hold your attention to the middle of the canvas or focal point.

11. Blossoms & Reflection
(No. 10 badger filbert)

Define the back petals, side petals and lower petals with **White**, sweeping from the outside toward the center. Do the same for the reflection under the one distant blossom.

12. Blossoms & Reflections
(No. 10 badger filbert)

Add **Dark Pink** (brush mix Alizarin Crimson + White) to the bottom of the petals, sweeping from the center of the flower outward. Do the same for the reflection under the one distant blossom.

13. Blossoms & Cupped Leaves
(No. 10 badger filbert)

Add a few more **White** foreshortened edge petals to give the flower volume and dimension. Use **Naples Yellow** to tap on speckled center stamens in the three lowest blossoms. Sweep **Pale Lavender** (brush mix White + a touch of Purple mix) contours on the cupped pad leaves from the valley or from the inside outward. Accent the edges of these same leaves.

Tip: Use more paint for the highlights on the closest lily pads for more rich and intense colors.

WATER LILY POND

Finishing Touches (Hake)

Mop the outer edges of the painting. Also mop the reflection only of the distant upper lily blossom. (See page 19 for an explanation of mopping.)

Wave & Light Patterns

WIND AND WATER have the relationship of professional dancers. Waves are orchestrated rhythmic movements of deep dark blues and translucent lights overlaid with the exquisite lace of foam patterns being stretched and pulled. I become mesmerized when watching the ever changing formations of waves with their energetic conflicts of troughs and crests.

This project doesn't need an acrylic black-to-gray value plan. Typically, I use a value plan to hold or lock down the important hard edges, detail or very dark value areas. A value study doesn't allow you to blend the details or shapes so much that you change their form. Although controlling the values is always important, waves are made with countless blended gradations or transitions of values, or basically, no hard edges. Among the things you'll learn with this painting is how to overlay and paint detailed foam patterns into the wet blended structure and values of the waves.

materials

SURFACE
Stretched Canvas, 12" × 16"
(30cm × 41cm)

ACRYLIC
Luminous Orange

OIL
Martin/F. Weber Permalba White -
1¾" (44mm)

Martin/F. Weber Prima Oil Colors
Ivory Black - ¾" (19mm)
Cobalt Blue - ½" (13mm)
Cadmium Red Light - a touch
Naples Yellow - ¼" (6mm)
Cobalt Violet - ¼" (6mm)

BRUSHES
Foam, 1-inch (25mm) (to apply
Luminous Orange)

Bristle, 1-inch (25mm)
(to apply medium)

Badger filbert, no.10

Hake, 1¾-inch (44mm)

OTHER MATERIALS
Robert Warren's Professional
Clear Medium

Palette knife (for mixing paint)

Wipe out tool

Pattern (see page 123)

1. Canvas Preparation

Prepare the canvas for the value painting as described on page 12. For this painting you will not create a value painting. Throughout this demonstration you'll find references to the parts of a wave that you see in the photo above. Please refer to the labeled drawing on page 123 for the terminology used for the parts of the wave in this demo.

2. Sky (No. 10 badger filbert)

Paint **Dark Teal** approximately 1" (25mm) down from the top of the canvas. Then stretch this color until it is 2" (51mm) down from the top of the canvas, working around the clouds.

DARK TEAL
½" (13mm) each of Ivory Black & Cobalt Blue + ¼" (6mm) White

MEDIUM TEAL
¼" (6mm) each of White & Dark Teal mix

PEACH
¼" (6mm) White + a touch each of Cadmium Red Light & Naples Yellow

CREAM
½" (13mm) White + ⅛" (3mm) Naples Yellow

PURPLE-GRAY
⅛" (3mm) each of White & Ivory Black + ¼" (6mm) Cobalt Violet

LAVENDER-GRAY
⅛" (3mm) each of Purple Gray mix & White

3. Sky (No. 10 badger filbert)

Overlap the Dark Teal with **Medium Teal**, stretching and blending this color lower between the clouds to about the middle of the sky area.

4. Sky (No. 10 badger filbert)

Starting in the lowest middle area between the clouds (not on the horizon), overwork with **Peach**, blending up into the Medium Teal and Dark Teal. Don't forget to blend up above the clouds on the left. Glaze over the low horizon line and stretched-out areas near the horizon (over orange canvas) and blend with horizontal strokes, moving upward to the base of the clouds.

5. Clouds (No. 10 badger filbert)

Work **Cream** into the center open space between the upper clouds to create the glow from the sun. Blend this into the open Peach and Medium Teal areas. Transition from the bright middle area into the previous colors. Add a touch of **White** to the brush for a lighter, brighter accent under the upper clouds. Blend smooth.

6. Clouds (No. 10 badger filbert)

Use **Purple-Gray** to scrub and blot in upper and lower cloud formations. Create staggered stretched-out low cloud formations, overlapping almost to the horizon line. Define the waterline and blend down about ½" (13mm) into the distant water, not going into the wave shapes.

7. Clouds (No. 10 badger filbert)

Loosely add **Dark Teal** to the darkest areas of all clouds. Use blotting and blending strokes to lightly add this color to the base of the low and middle clouds, creating bottom impressions.

8. Clouds (No. 10 badger filbert)

With a wipe out tool, wipe out the left side of the right cloud to expose touches of orange canvas.

9. Clouds (No. 10 badger filbert)

Add a touch of **Peach** to highlight, blending into the clouds. Using the brush edge, add very thin stretched-out highlights around the open spaces in the clouds above the horizon. If necessary, re-accent the lightest glowing area with **Cream**.

10. Wave (No. 10 badger filbert)

Base in the dark areas and other trough areas with **Dark Teal.** Stroke with the chisel edge of the brush, striving to capture the movement of the water. Don't worry about covering the pattern lines.

11. Wave (No. 10 badger filbert)

Blend up into window of large wave with **Medium Teal.**

12. Wave (No. 10 badger filbert)

With **Cream**, blend higher into the large wave and along the crest, sloping toward the right. Also add to the top of the lower crest.

13. Wave (No. 10 badger filbert)

Blend the **Cream** down into the Medium Teal.

14. Wave (No. 10 badger filbert)

Use your pattern to retrace the foam lines into the wet paint (see "Tracing Pattern Lines on Oils," page 12).

15. Wave (No. 10 badger filbert)

Use a brush mix of **Purple-Gray** and **Medium Teal** to create contrasting foam patterns on the top of the large wave, tapering down into the wave's middle value. Use the brush tip to create shapes that start wide and then taper. Also add horizontal movements to the distant water.

16. Wave (No. 10 badger filbert)

Go over traced lines with **Lavender-Gray** to create foam patterns. Scoop the paint up on the tip of brush and use delicate to heavy strokes to create thin-to-wide shapes. Leave various-sized elliptical openings, all flowing with the contours of the waves. Frequently wipe off the brush on a paper towel and reload with clean color. Keep perspective in mind, making smaller foam patterns as you go into the distance.

17. Wave (No. 10 badger filbert)

Add several **Lavender-Gray** crests in the distant horizon area, using thin strokes. Work larger movements off the sides and bottom of the canvas. This color should blend into the base color of the water, creating subtle variations and contrasts. Restate dark elliptical patterns if necessary.

18. Wave (No. 10 badger filbert)

Scoop **Cream** on the brush tip and add very thin highlights to the distant crests and small wisps or splashes above the window of the large wave. Accent a few sloping contours to the left side of the smaller right wave. Emphasize the top and right slopes of the closest wave crest. Allow the paint texture to show for better definition. Frequently wipe off the brush and reload with clean paint. If necessary, restate the translucent window of the large wave.

19. Wave (No. 10 badger filbert)

Create a sparkling effect by accenting the brightest foam highlights with **White**.

WAVE & LIGHT PATTERNS

Finishing Touches (1¾-inch [44mm] Hake)

With a hake brush, gently mop the foam in the trough areas of the waves, being careful not to eliminate the brightest highlights. Besides eliminating brushstrokes, this blends out any "pressed-in" pattern lines that might still be showing. Also carefully mop the clouds and sky. (See page 19 for an explanation of mopping.)

Bridge to
Upper Falls

 **JUST AN HOUR FROM MY STUDIO,** the beautiful Hocking Hills region in Ohio has a special area known as Old Man's Cave. Hidden in the hills are amazing natural rock formations and gorges carved by streams over millions of years. This is a favorite place for my students and me to paint on location. Many students comment that they never expected to see or paint anything like this in Ohio. The timeless beauty of the area has been passed on from ancient to present cultures. As I paint these colorful rocks and dark, emerald-green waters, I can almost hear the voices of the Native Americans who lived there hundreds of years earlier.

One of the biggest challenges for a landscape painter is depicting realistic rocks. This painting gives you plenty of practice toward developing that skill. The light in it is typical of midday when the sun is straight up, highlighting the deepest parts of the stream and gorge. Nevertheless, this is a "low key" painting—a painting with a dominance of dark values. In this case, I find a solid, flat black acrylic base to be the most advantageous for establishing the dark values in the rocks and water.

materials

1. Canvas Preparation & Sky (1-inch [25mm] foam brush & no. 10 badger filbert)

Apply flat black acrylic paint to the entire canvas with a 1-inch (25mm) foam brush. Let dry. Transfer the pattern using white transfer paper. Apply Professional Clear Medium as described on page 17.

Paint open sky with **Lavender-Blue**, working around the tree shapes, above and below the bridge arch and into a few sky holes between trees. Create a brush mix of **Light Turquoise** (¼" [6mm] White + a touch of Turquoise) in a value that is lighter than the Lavender-Blue. Add this mix to the middle of the open sky and above and below the bridge. Blend into the Lavender-Blue.

LAVENDER-BLUE
¼" (6mm) White + a touch each of Cobalt Blue & Cobalt Violet

DARK GREEN
¼" (6mm) each of Cobalt Blue & Burnt Umber

MEDIUM GREEN
¼" (6mm) White + ⅛" (3mm) each of Dark Green mix & Sap Green

PURPLE-GRAY
⅛" (3mm) White + ¼" (6mm) Cobalt Violet + ⅛" (3mm) Ivory Black

MAUVE
½" (13mm) White + ⅛" (3mm) each of Burnt Sienna & Cadmium Red Medium

2. Foliage (No. 10 badger filbert)

Use **Dark Green** to glaze over all foliage above the bridge and very thinly under the bridge. Lightly work the foliage edges into the sky color. Using a foliage stroke, tap **Medium Green** onto all the foliage, creating dimensional leaf "clumps." Slightly soften by tapping the edges of the trees into the sky color.

3. Slopes & Streambed (No. 10 badger filbert)

Add **Burnt Sienna** background slopes to the distant hillside under the arch. Add **Purple-Gray** to the rocky streambed above the waterfall and blend into the slopes.

4. Rocks & Water (No. 10 badger filbert)

Using **Lavender-Gray** (brush mix White + Purple Gray), create subtle definition to the tops of the streambed rocks. With **Light Turquoise** (brush mix ¼" [6mm] White + a touch of Turquoise), add small highlight touches to the water falling between the rocks.

5. Tree Trunks (No. 10 badger filbert)

Suggest some **Dark Green** distant tree trunks over the background slopes.

ORANGE
¼" (6mm) White + ⅛" (3mm)
each of Cadmium Yellow
Light & Cadmium Red Light

YELLOW-GREEN
⅛" (3mm) each of White
& Sap Green + ¼" (6mm)
Naples Yellow

6. Bridge, Rocks & Water (No. 10 badger filbert)

Throughout this step, use very deliberate strokes of **Burnt Umber** to create the many facets, angles and edges of the rocks. Do not blend. Utilize the black canvas for darker values in crevasses and shadows. Blot rock impressions on the side of the bridge. Glaze under the arch of the bridge with curved contouring strokes. Add first values to many rock shapes on the right and left sides of the painting. Add a few touches into the darker areas of water at the bottom of the canvas.

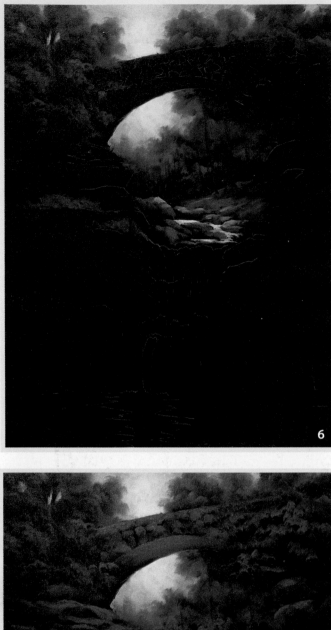

7. Bridge, Rocks & Water (No. 10 badger filbert)

Add a few touches of **Raw Sienna** to the smaller stones on the side of the bridge. Blend in a reflected light under the curve of the arch. Add deliberate planes and surface angles to the tops of the waterfall rocks, stroking in the color. With a single firm stroke, eliminate the bottom edge of the previous stroke by overlapping the bottom edge and blending into the rock. Include a few touches of this color in the dark water shadows to suggest underwater rocks. Use **Mauve** to selectively highlight the areas you just painted with Raw Sienna.

8. Bridge, Rocks & Water (No. 10 badger filbert)

Add a few touches of mossy **Medium Green** to the stones beside the bridge and a few strokes to the shaded slopes of the rocks. Keep deliberate planes and angles by stroking in the color and blending it into the rocks. Using the foliage stroke, create loose overlapping foliage on bridge's side. Stroke the color horizontally in the water pool. Use **Dark Green** to restate any dark values in the rock crevasses or shadows. Add horizontal sweeping strokes to the water pool from the outside edges toward the middle, blending slightly with Medium Green.

9. Bridge & Rocks (No. 10 badger filbert)

Use **Orange** to accent a few stones on the side of the bridge. Add a brighter reflected light under the arch of the bridge. Selectively highlight a few rocks near the center of the painting (highlights should face the waterfall) to create a brighter focal point. Use **Naples Yellow** to create the brightest light on the rocks facing the waterfall, accenting as if the light is coming from above. Also add small highlights to the stone "bumps" on the top edge of the bridge. Be very selective with this color. Use less paint in the brush and overwork (or tap stroke twice), for a dull distant highlight on the rocks in the distant stream.

10. Foliage & Water (No. 10 badger filbert)

Using the foliage stroke, blot **Sap Green** loosely into the right- and left-side foliage overlapping the bridge. Don't fill in too much. Add a touch into the distant trees. Add a very few touches between the rocks and a few horizontal strokes in the water pool. Use **Yellow-Green** and a foliage stroke to add lacy, loose leaves and leaf clumps, some overhanging the rocks. Work a few smaller touches on the distant trees. Add just a few horizontal strokes to the water pool.

11. Foliage Highlights (No. 10 badger filbert)

Use a very few touches of **Cadmium Yellow Light** to highlight leaves of the foliage overhanging the rocks.

12. Waterfall & Mist (No. 10 badger filbert)

Add sweeping **Purple-Gray** strokes from the top of the waterfall down in tapering shapes. On the lowest landing above pool, add a misty area by blotting and blending.

13. Waterfall & Mist (No. 10 badger filbert)

Highlight the falling water and mist with **Lavender-Gray** (brush mix Purple-Gray + White). Further highlight the falling water and mist with **Lavender-Blue**, being careful not to totally cover the previous colors.

14. Water Pool (No. 10 badger filbert)

Add **Turquoise** to the center of the pool with horizontal strokes, streaking and sweeping into the sides.

15. Waterfall (No. 10 badger filbert)

Highlight the tops of the waterfalls with **White**. Then pull the color down, using dragging and skipping strokes to simulate the falling water. Stop your vertical strokes at the water pool. Then scoop paint on the brush tip and add choppy horizontal splash marks where the waterfall hits the pool. Add horizontal water ripples in the center of the pool. Add White accents to the distant water trickles in the stream.

**BRIDGE TO
UPPER FALLS**

Finishing Touches (Hake)

Mop the water pool horizontally and soften the rock edges on the outer sides of canvas.
Mop the distant background trees and sky, staying away from the "chunky," thicker paint
of the closer leaves. (See page 19 for an explanation of mopping.)

Floral Garden Reflections

IF YOU DON'T HAVE THE PERFECT photo for a painting project — create one. By combining elements from different photos, I was able to create this pleasing composition. The picturesque setting demonstrates natural perspective with color and atmosphere. Mixing subtle elements of poetic and rhythmic water rings with the high contrast of the white roses against dark foliage and reflections, creates a scene similar to the pre-Raphaelite style of the late 1800s to early 1900s. Notice how the vertical arborvitae bushes offer a touch of formality while the elliptical water rings evoke a subliminal calming effect.

The perspective is largely carried with the distant, middle and close floral textures and their related reflections. Painting and understanding the black acrylic value study is an important step for this project. Notice how the large dark foliage mass near the middle and on the right, and the two smaller vertical shapes on the left, create a well-balanced composition. Also note the placement of the foreground dark rose foliage against the light areas of the water and the lighter foliage and white roses in front of the darker reflections. This is a good example of how cool colors recede and warm colors come forward. This painting also presents more than the usual challenge with vertical water distortions and horizontal surface movements.

materials

SURFACE

Stretched Canvas, 12" × 16"
   (30cm × 41cm)

ACRYLIC

Luminous Orange

Flat Black

OIL

Martin/F. Weber Permalba White
   - 1¼" (31mm)

Martin/F. Weber Prima Oil Colors
   Cobalt Blue - ¾" (19mm)
   Cadmium Yellow Medium
      - ⅛" (3mm)
   Cobalt Violet - ¼" (6mm)
   Burnt Umber - ¼" (6mm)
   Sap Green - ½" (13mm)
   Naples Yellow - a touch
   Cadmium Red Light - ⅛" (3mm)
   Prima Pink - ⅛" (3mm)

BRUSHES

Foam, 1-inch (25mm)
   (to apply Luminous Orange)

Bristle, 1-inch (25mm)
   (to apply medium)

Synthetic flat, ¼-inch (6mm)
   & ½-inch (13mm)

Stiff bristle, no. 10

Badger filbert, no. 10

Hake, 1¾-inch (44mm)

OTHER MATERIALS

Robert Warren's Professional
   Clear Medium

Palette knife (for mixing paint)

Pattern (see page 124)

Pencil (to retrace water rings)

1. Value Painting (¼-inch [6mm] & ½-inch [13mm] synthetic flats)

Prepare the canvas for the value painting as described on page 12. When transferring the pattern, don't trace the circular water rings (they will be transferred later). Use flat black acrylic for the value painting, alternating between the ½-inch (13mm) synthetic flat for larger areas and the ¼-inch (6mm) synthetic flat for more detailed areas (see pages 13-17 for value-painting techniques).

Paint horizontally to define the water edge. Working up from the waterline, tap in rows of foliage impressions, leaving open orange texture for blossoms at the top of each row. Control your values with the amount of paint in the brush to separate the foliage layers (see page 14). Each layer should be darker at the bottom and become lighter toward the top.

Use the brush corner and black (dark value) paint to define the loose top outline of the highlight bush foliage on the right.

Work the tree shapes up to the top of the canvas, keeping loose edges and leaving open sky areas. Create vertical texture to the two tall,

narrow trees on the left and add corresponding reflections.

Define distant tree foliage impressions by defining the base first. Then with a drier brush, work up to gray values. Don't forget to work through or behind the two tall, narrow tree shapes on the left.

For contrast against the dark reflections, sharply define and paint around all the foreground white roses and lower right rose leaf shapes. Paint in a few dark leaf shapes against the light water reflection area on the left and center of the lower canvas.

With both broad and narrow strokes, pull down vertical reflections from the edge of the water, working carefully around the rose shapes in the foreground.

With a dry brush, add gray tones to leaf foliage on the right side foreground.

Allow the black acrylic value painting to dry. Apply Professional Clear Medium as described on page 17.

LIGHT BLUE
¼" (6mm) White +⅛"
(3mm) Cobalt Blue

CREAM
¼" (6mm) White + touch of
Cadmium Yellow Medium

LAVENDER-BLUE
¼" (6mm) White + ⅛"
(3mm) each of Cobalt Blue
& Cobalt Violet

LAVENDER
¼" (6mm) White + ⅛"
(3mm) Cobalt Violet

2. Sky & Sky Reflections (No. 10 stiff bristle brush)

Blot **Light Blue** into the open spaces of the sky, working around the treetops. With vertical and horizontal strokes, add sky reflections in the water toward the bottom of the canvas, working between and around the flower shapes. Don't worry about covering the water rings. Accent the lowest horizon area of the sky with **Cream**, working into the Light Blue. Then, using vertical and horizontal strokes, add Cream sky reflections in the water, allowing your strokes to blend into the Light Blue and working around the dark reflections.

3. Reflections (No. 10 stiff bristle brush)

Using vertical and horizontal strokes, pull **Lavender-Blue** up from the bottom of the canvas, allowing it to blend into the previous colors and working around the flower shapes. (Don't worry if you paint over some of the leaves a bit; you can easily reinstate them later.)

4. Distant Hill, Reflections & Foliage (No. 10 badger filbert)

Loosely define the top profile of the distant hill with **Lavender**. Also work the color between the tree shapes. Use the corner of the brush to add a few touches to the edges of the tall trees on the right. Loosely apply some of this color to the lower edges of the foliage reflections. With **Lavender-Blue**, create the more distant tree foliage profile, overlapping and working in and out of the Lavender you just applied. Add Lavender-Blue foliage reflections to the water, using vertical and horizontal strokes.

DARK GREEN
¼" (6mm) each of Burnt Umber & Cobalt Blue

MEDIUM GREEN
⅛" (3mm) each of Dark Green mix & White & Sap Green & Cobalt Blue

YELLOW-GREEN
⅛" (3mm) each of White & Sap Green

5. Foliage, Reflections, Trees & Grass (No. 10 badger filbert)

Glaze over all the dark foliage areas with **Dark Green**. Then use the tip of the brush to create lacy edges of leafy texture on the tree foliage against the sky and vertical texture on the tall trees on the left. Glaze over the dark areas of the reflections and over the light-value rosebush leaves in the lower right corner. Use **Medium Green** to create dimensional foliage clumps within the dark areas of the tall right trees and lower into the middle and right bush foliage. Add vertical texture to the trees on the left. Suggest distant grass impressions. Add to foliage reflections in the water, using vertical and horizontal strokes.

6. Grass & Trees (No. 10 badger filbert)

Use **Mint Green** (brush mix White + just a speck of Yellow-Green and Medium Green mixes) to highlight the trees with foliage strokes. Highlight the tall trees on the left with light vertical touches (see step 5 detail above). Add a touch of this color to the left grassy area and then lightly add it to the foliage reflections in the water. Add **Yellow-Green** to the highest line of bush foliage in front of the trees on the right. There should be more highlighting as you move into the lighter area in the middle of the painting. Add a touch of the same color to the right side of the distant meadow and to the foliage reflection in the water. Add a few **Naples Yellow** touches to the same foliage areas where you applied Yellow-Green and to the right side of the distant meadow. Do not add this color to the reflections.

7. Flowers & Reflections (No. 10 badger filbert)

Add **Cobalt Violet** to the undersides and middles of all the flower clumps across the entire painting. Loosely blot this color into the dark and middle-value areas of the bushes, using the foliage stroke. Add vertical and horizontal reflections in the water. Tap **Cadmium Red Light** on the blossoms on the middle and right bushes. Slightly overwork the paint into the shadows for a dull color. Add sparingly to the reflections. Loosely add **Lavender** into the top edges of the left flower shapes. Add vertical and horizontal reflections in the water.

8. Flowers & Reflections (No. 10 badger filbert)

Add **Prima Pink** flowers, starting very sparingly with smaller shapes in the distant purple flower bushes. Then apply this color on the left edge and in the middle of the pink flower bushes. Note that these flower textures are in larger clumps. Overwork this color for a dull touch to the reflections. Add just a few **Cream** accents to the middle area of the flowers. Do not add Cream to the reflections.

9. Flower Foliage & Reflections (No. 10 badger filbert)

Loosely add a little **Medium Green** foliage to the dark areas between and under the flower bushes, working from the center to the right area of the canvas. Loosely highlight a few leaves in the flower foliage with **Yellow-Green**. Add a touch of this color to the closest reflections. Add a few **Naples Yellow** accents to the edge of the closest clump of flowers.

10. Mop, Restate Rose Leaves & Stems (Hake & No. 10 badger filbert)

With the hake brush, mop the background trees and lightly blot into the dark shadows of the flowers and the background foliage. Then carefully mop the water, using horizontal strokes. With the no. 10 badger filbert, add **Dark Green** to restate the darkest silhouetted leaves and stems of the close roses on the lower right and left side.

11. Rose Foliage (No. 10 badger filbert)

Using **Medium Green**, glaze the remaining leaf shapes on the rosebushes in the lower right. Add a few **Sap Green** strokes to the rosebush leaves to emphasize a richer color. Selectively add **Yellow-Green** highlight accents to the tops of a few leaves. Splash on just a few **Cadmium Yellow Medium** accents.

12. Roses (No. 10 badger filbert)

Base in the roses with a glaze of **Lavender** over the orange acrylic. Shade the inside and bottom petals of the blossoms with **Lavender-Blue**. Define three background petals stroking downward and one or two saucer petals with **White**, stroking upward. Then stroke White on a couple of angular edge petals cutting through the middle of the blossoms (see step 13 detail below).

Step 13 Detail

13. Water Rings (Pattern & Pencil)

Overlay the pattern sheet on the wet painting and retrace the water rings with a pencil (as described in "Tracing Pattern Lines on Oils" on page 12). Notice that the elliptical shapes of the water rings are extremely horizontal from end to end. The rings will be made with both light and dark values.

14. Water Rings & Horizontal Movement (No. 10 badger filbert)

Use the tip of a no. 10 badger filbert and **Cream** to very lightly suggest water rings. Start in the lightest area of the water reflections and sweep into and through the dark reflections. Wipe out the brush before beginning another ring. Working between the Cream rings, add strokes of **Purple-Gray** (brush mix Lavender Blue + touch of Cobalt Violet) in the darkest reflection area of the ripples, sweeping out from the dark into the light background reflections. Add a few **Lavender-Blue** horizontal water movements to the surface of the distant and middle water.

FLORAL GARDEN REFLECTIONS

Finishing Touches (Hake)

Horizontally mop water rings and ripples. Be sure to wipe the brush off on a paper towel between strokes. (See page 19 for an explanation of mopping.)

Snowy Blue Run Creek

WHEN I WAS A KID in the country, my favorite playground was the creek. Through the seasons it offered different activities, from swimming to skating, and there was always an adventure to be had there. I waded through the water to visit friends over the next hill. In the winter my brother and I took turns pulling each other over the ice with a sled—one of our favorite activities, even though we sometimes fell through and froze our pant legs.

As an adult, I find the creek holds an attraction as a painting subject. In this project, you have the challenges of creating a distant glowing light through winter trees, long cool shadows of blue from evening light, watery distortions of reflected trees and horizontal movements from a slight winter breeze.

materials

SURFACE
Stretched Canvas, 12" × 16"
(30cm × 41cm)

ACRYLIC
Luminous Orange

Flat Black

OIL
Martin/F. Weber Permalba White
- 2" (51mm)

Martin/F. Weber Prima Oil Colors
Cadmium Yellow Light
- ¼" (6mm)
Cobalt Blue - ¾" (19mm)
Cobalt Violet - ½" (13mm)
Ivory Black - ¼" (6mm)
Turquoise - ⅛" (3mm)
Burnt Umber - ¼" (6mm)

BRUSHES
Foam, 1-inch (25mm) (to apply
Luminous Orange)

Bristle, 1-inch (25mm)
(to apply medium)

Synthetic flat, ¼-inch (6mm) &
½-inch (13mm)

Badger filbert, no.10

Hake, 1¾-inch (44mm)

OTHER MATERIALS
Robert Warren's Professional
Clear Medium

Palette knife (for mixing paint)

Pattern (see page 124)

1

1. Value Painting (½-inch [13mm] & ¼-inch [6mm] synthetic flats)

Prepare the canvas for the value painting as described on page 12. Use flat black acrylic for the value painting (see pages 13-17 for value-painting techniques). Start in the foreground and work into the distance.

With a ½-inch (13mm) synthetic flat, paint the large tree trunk, creating bark with vertical texture. Use a drier brush for lighter (more orange) values on the left half of the trunk. Loosely add tree trunk shadows, rock "lumps and bumps" and roughage to the foreground bank gently sloping toward the water. Outline the creek bank. Paint in the middle-range tree trunks by using vertical edge strokes. Then

suggest specific tree trunk reflections in the water with a wavy tapered line.

Using a ¼-inch (6mm) synthetic flat, create distant tree trunk impressions. Add the dark mass of distant trees with their short reflections on the far edge of the water. Create contours and shadows on the sloping banks. Using a drier brush and a short vertical scrubbing motion, create the foliage in the distance with a few tree trunks.

Tip: Dark values get lighter in the distance. Light values get darker or dull in the distance

Allow the black acrylic to dry. Apply Professional Clear Medium as described on page 17.

CREAM	**LIGHT BLUE**	**LAVENDER-BLUE**	**PURPLE-GRAY**	**BLUE-GRAY**
¼" (6mm) White + a touch of Cadmium Yellow Light	½" (13mm) White + ⅛" (3mm) Cobalt Blue	½" (13mm) White + ⅛" (3mm) each of Cobalt Blue & Cobalt Violet	¼" (6mm) each of White & Ivory Black & Cobalt Violet	¼" (6mm) Purple Gray mix + ⅛" (3mm) Cobalt Blue

2. Sky & Water (No. 10 badger filbert)

Blot **Cream** into the lightest area of the distant sky. Add vertical streaks to the water to suggest corresponding reflections. Working out from the Cream area, add **Light Blue** to the sky. Also add vertically stroked reflections, working into the Cream. Add **Lavender-Blue** to the outer edges of the sky, working out to the left and right sides of the canvas. Then apply this color in vertical strokes to the water area, working from the foreground bank and sweeping up into the middle reflections. Scatter a little of all three colors here and there through the trees to indicate the sky showing through.

3. Trees, Water & Tree Reflections (No. 10 badger filbert)

Use **Purple-Gray** to loosely blot in the top shapes of the distant trees and the upper foliage on the right and left sides of the canvas and down toward the distant ground. Glaze over the lower dark base of the distant trees. Use the brush edge to suggest tree trunks. Glaze over the water edge and add tree reflections with vertical strokes. Vary your strokes from long to short, working from the water edge downward. Darken the bottom of the distant trees and their reflections with **Blue-Gray**. Also darken the tree reflections on the closest water banks, working from the water edge down. Suggest more trunks on the distant bank, working all the way to the left and right sides of the canvas.

4. Sky & Water (No. 10 badger filbert)

If necessary, restate the brightest area of the sky and water with **Cream**. Also if necessary, blot **Light Blue** in between distant trees as well as their water reflections.

AQUA
¼" (6mm) White + ⅛" (3mm) each of Cadmium Yellow Light & Turquoise

DARK GREEN
⅛" (3mm) each of Burnt Umber & Cobalt Blue

5. Distant Snowbanks (No. 10 badger filbert)

Add **Light Blue** to the tops of the distant snowbanks. You may stroke right over the tree trunks.

6. Distant Snowbanks (No. 10 badger filbert)

With **Lavender-Blue**, create shadow contours of distant snow, working down to the creek edge.

7. Distant Snowbanks (No. 10 badger filbert)

Thinly apply **White** to the snow, making the tops of the distant snowbanks brighter and working downward for a bluer (duller) color.

8. Foreground & Mid-Ground Snow (No. 10 badger filbert)

Add **Blue-Gray** to the darkest shadows of all foreground and mid-ground snow, including the large tree trunk shadow. Define the edge of the creek banks and the ice along the banks.

9. Foreground & Mid-Ground Snow (No. 10 badger filbert)

Work **Lavender-Blue** in and out of the edges of the darker Blue-Gray shadows. Also add "lumps and bumps" in the snow at the bottom of the canvas and in the area left of the large tree trunk.

10. Snow & Ice (No. 10 badger filbert)

Add wide strokes of **Aqua** to the right side of the snow lumps and the left side of the large tree. Add small touches to the distant snowbanks. Also apply this color loosely to show reflected light on the shadows of the foreground bank and ice.

11. Snow & Ice Highlights & Accents (No. 10 badger filbert)

Add **Cream** snow highlights to the foreground terrain and ice and on a few mounds on the middle-distant banks. Blend gently into the shadows. Wipe off the brush frequently with a paper towel and replenish with clean color. Accent the cream highlights with **White**.

12. Middle Trees & Their Reflections (No. 10 badger filbert)

Using the brush edge, define all the middle-distant tree trunks and limbs and their corresponding reflections with **Brownish Gray** (brush mix Blue-Gray mix + Burnt Umber). Do not work on the distant trees.

13. Trees, Shadows & Reflections
(No. 10 badger filbert)

Glaze over the large tree trunk with **Burnt Umber**. Define the branches and accent the darker right side of this trunk with **Dark Green**. Also accent the darkest shadows in the foreground, the edges of the ice and banks, and the dark right sides of the closest middle trees and their reflections.

14. Large Tree & Shadows
(No. 10 badger filbert)

Add **Lavender-Blue** bark texture to the middle of the large tree trunk. Blend this color at the base of the trunk into the ground. Apply some of this color to the top of the limbs where the snow will be. Add a few touches of **Aqua** into the shadows on the side and middle of the large tree trunks and limbs.

15. Tree Accents
(No. 10 badger filbert)

Using the brush edge and **White**, accent the bark texture on the left side of the large tree trunk and limbs. Also accent a few middle-distant tree trunks.

16. Ripples & Tree Shadows (No. 10 badger filbert)

Thinly add a few **Lavender-Blue** horizontal ripple lines, sweeping from the creek banks inward. Then stroke in the middle-distance tree shadows.

SNOWY BLUE RUN CREEK

Finishing Touches (Hake)

Mop the tops of the middle and distant trees. Mop the large tree lightly, leaving the texture. Mop the snow, following the contours. (See page 19 for an explanation of mopping.)

Big Thompson River Canyon

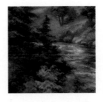 **I'M SURE I'M NOT ALONE** when I say that I'm attracted to any type of water. Particularly intriguing is pausing at a higher elevation to look down over beautiful vistas. On one particular day I found myself on a small dirt road just west of Loveland, Colorado, probably two hundred feet above the Big Thompson River. The rippled patterns of the moving water from this unusual perspective intrigued me. I had to capture them. So I quickly set up my plein–air easel and began sketching and painting. I become very excited and focused when painting on location. I remember one foot slipping toward the edge a few times and dealing with a sore hip the next day from standing on an uneven cliffside.

This painting introduces the effect of water bouncing off both sides of a rock-lined gorge, creating ripple patterns that continuously cross over and through each other. The dramatic perspective goes from almost-level water movements near the horizon line to the diagonal crisscross patterns almost straight down. You'll only encounter this combination one way—from a high elevation.

materials

1. Value Painting (¼-inch [6mm] & ½-inch [13mm] synthetic flats)

Prepare the canvas for the value painting as described on page 12. Use flat black acrylic for the value painting alternating between the ½-inch (12mm) synthetic flat for larger areas and the ¼-inch (6mm) synthetic flat for more detailed areas (see pages 13-17 for value-painting techniques).

Define the tree trunks in the lower left group of trees and on the opposite side of the water. Blot and scrub the darkest areas, leaving a little orange base color showing for highlights. Using the corner of the brush with the foliage stroke, define the right side of the foliage detail and the pine tops.

At the trees' base, paint solid black around the large lower left rock. Paint in the foreground rock by adding shaded right slopes and lighter highlight (dry-brush) slopes on the top.

Underline the opposite water edge with black (darkest value). Sweep dark values horizontally from the right river edge toward the left side working from flat to more diagonal strokes. Now tap and sweep from the left edge toward the right, following the ripple pattern contours .

Add right-side rock shapes by painting negative spaces between the rock shapes. Define the top profile of the right mountain and its cracks and crevices. With the brush corner, add distant foliage along the low slope profile of the right mountain. Add clumps of sagebrush and shadows on the slopes and between the rocks. Work into the distant mountainsides on the upper left and define the profiles and slopes of the mountains. Create light and dark terrain and foliage impressions sloping toward the right mountain. Allow the black acrylic value painting to dry. Apply Professional Clear Medium as described on page 17.

MEDIUM BLUE	**LIGHT BLUE**	**CREAM**	**PURPLE-GRAY**
½" (13mm) White + ⅛" (3mm) each of Cobalt Blue & Cobalt Violet	¼" (6mm) White + a touch of Cobalt Blue	½" (13mm) White + a touch of Naples Yellow	¼" (6mm) White + ¼" (6mm) each of Ivory Black & Cobalt Violet

2. Sky (No. 10 badger filbert & hake)

Apply **Medium Blue** to the upper sky. Add **Light Blue** to the lower sky above the mountains, blending up into the Medium Blue. Blot in **Cream** cloud shapes in a general diagonal direction. With the hake brush, lightly mop the clouds and sky together.

3. Distant Mountains (No. 10 badger filbert)

Glaze **Purple-Gray** over the most distant mountain. To suggest light on the left side of the peaks and ridges, add **White** to the brush, creating a slightly lighter value. Use **Blue-Gray** to define the profile of the closer left mountain. Also brush this color downward on the slope, stopping as it meets the right hillside and goes behind the tall left pine tree.

4. Right Hillside (No. 10 badger filbert)

Glaze the hillside and the rocky cliff on the right with **Purple-Gray**. Work around the three hillside trees. Use **Dark Green** to add the bush, tree foliage shapes, and the tree trunks. Work this darker value down between the lower rocks along the river. Also accent the darker values on the edges of the water and between the rocks.

BLUE-GRAY
⅛" (3mm) each of Purple-Gray mix & Medium Blue mix

DARK GREEN
¼" (6mm) each of Burnt Umber & Cobalt Blue

MEDIUM GREEN
⅛" (3mm) each of Ivory Black & White & Cobalt Blue

BURNT ORANGE
¼" (6mm) White + ⅛" (3mm) each of Cadmium Red Light & Cadmium Yellow Medium & Burnt Sienna

LIGHT GOLD
¼" (6mm) White + a touch of Cadmium Yellow Medium

YELLOW-GREEN
¼" (6mm) each of Sap Green & White

5. Foliage & Left Hillside (No.10 badger filbert)

Using a foliage stroke and **Medium Green**, blot in the inner foliage shapes of the trees and bushes on the hillside and cliff. Add a slight touch to the distant left hillside. Shade the right side of the foliage with **Blue-Gray**.

6. Water (No. 10 badger filbert)

Glaze **Dark Green** over the dark areas of the water, specifically, the tree reflections and the water at the base of the cliff. Lightly glaze **Medium Green** over the lighter areas of water between the tree reflections. Glaze **Purple-Gray** over the water at the bottom of the canvas, blending up to the middle of the canvas.

7. Water (No. 10 badger filbert)

With **Medium Blue**, make vertical and horizontal strokes working from the most distant water into the middle water area. Be sure to work this color in and out of the rock edges. Then, starting in the mid-distance, use very little paint to add crossing contour lines of water ripples (see sidebar at right), curving left and right and diminishing toward the bottom of the canvas. Use **Light Blue** to add horizontal lines to the distant and middle water areas. Also add highlights to the Medium Blue ripples.

CROSSING CONTOUR RIPPLES

For all crossing contour ripples (step 7), paint continuous lines with a series of taps.

8. Cliffs & Hillsides (No. 10 badger filbert)

Add **Burnt Orange** slope contours to the hillside, working around the foliage. Also add highlights to the cliffs on the upper right and to the lower rocks. Add sloping angles and planes to the rocks along the edge of the water, but don't add as many to rocks in the lower right corner. Finally, add this color to the slope contours on the distant left hillside, gently overworking for a duller color. Apply **Naples Yellow** highlights to the same areas of slopes, rocks, cliffs and right hillsides. Use just a touch on the distant left hillside for a slightly duller color.

9. Gold Accents (No. 10 badger filbert)

Use **Light Gold** to accent the rocks and create a light focal point around the largest tree on the right. Also accent the slopes, rocks, cliff and hillsides (near and distant).

10. Right Hillside & Trees (No. 10 badger filbert & hake)

Add a touch of **Yellow-Green** into the slopes and the foliage of the near and distant right hillside. Overwork the color on the distant hillside to dull it a bit. Accent the trees on the near hillside with **Naples Yellow**, scooping the paint up. Make the color brightest on the nearest tree and overwork it a bit on the two trees further back for a duller color. With a hake, mop the water and all the land and rock areas, avoiding the closest tree on the right to preserve its texture.

11. Evergreens (No. 10 badger filbert)

Scrub in a **Dark Green** glaze over the left mass of evergreens. Define the tops and foliage against the water and redefine the trunks and limbs. Loosely blot **Sap Green** into the separate tops of the closer trees.

12. Evergreens (No. 10 badger filbert)

Place middle values of **Medium Green** to define the individual evergreens and the branch shapes within the evergreen mass. Add a few loose touches in the dark areas. Add a slight reflected light of **Medium Blue** to the shadowed right sides of the evergreens. Also use this color to define the tops of the lower trees. Use **Yellow-Green** to highlight the evergreens and to accent their tops on the left. Restate the darks with **Dark Green** if necessary.

13. Lower Left Rock (No. 10 badger filbert)

Glaze **Burnt Sienna** into the top and side slopes of the large rock on the lower left. Stroke **Purple-Gray** into the shadowed areas, working into the slope of the rock. Add a first highlight of **Burnt Orange** to create the shapes of the rock planes.

14. Rocks, Hillside & Cliff (No. 10 badger filbert)

Add a second highlight of **Naples Yellow**. Then add an accent of **Peach** to the top edge of the rock. At this time, also accent the rocks, hillside and cliff on the right side of the painting, focusing the brightest area in the middle of the canvas.

15. Rocks (No. 10 badger filbert)

Returning to the large rock on the left, add **Medium Blue** reflected light to the shaded right face. Then work the color into the crevasses of the rocks on the right side of the painting. If necessary, use **Dark Green** to restate the shadowed edges, cracks and crevices of the rocks and the right hillside tree trunks.

16. Water Shimmers (No. 10 badger filbert)

Scoop paint on the tip of the brush and add horizontal **Cream** water shimmers in the distance. In the mid- and foreground, skip and hit along the crisscross pattern of the ripple contours. Use **White** to accent the Cream water shimmers in the distance.

16

BIG THOMPSON RIVER CANYON

Finishing Touches (Hake)

Use the hake brush to lightly mop the water. Also blot mop the dark areas of the lower left tree foliage. Do not mop the left rock. Be sure to wipe the brush out on a paper towel between strokes. (See page 19 for an explanation of mopping.)

Rocky Mountain River

AFTER TEACHING a four-day indoor workshop in Colorado, I spent some extra time exploring the beautiful nearby Big Thompson and Cache la Poudre canyons. Both have rivers flowing down the eastern slopes of the Rocky Mountains. An artist and fly fisherman's paradise, the water runs cold and clear.

Looking down into this river offers the challenge of painting what you see at the bottom of the riverbed. Rocks abound, as they might take hundreds of years to tumble just a few feet. This painting shows how the dark reflections of trees on the right and left banks block out the sky's light reflections, allowing you to see the many underwater rocks with an illusion of much detail.

materials

SURFACE
Stretched Canvas, 12" × 16"
   (30cm × 41cm)

ACRYLIC
Luminous Orange

Flat Black

OIL
Martin/F. Weber Permalba White
   - 2" (51mm)

Martin/F. Weber Prima Oil Colors
   Cobalt Blue - ¾" (19mm)
   Cobalt Violet - ¼" (6mm)
   Ivory Black - ¼" (6mm)
   Prima Gray - ⅛" (3mm)
   Naples Yellow - ¼" (6mm)
   Burnt Umber - ½" (13mm)
   Sap Green - ¼" (6mm)
   Burnt Sienna - ⅛" (3mm)

BRUSHES
Foam, 1-inch (25mm) (to apply
   Luminous Orange)

Bristle, 1-inch (25mm)
   (to apply medium)

Synthetic flat, ¼-inch (6mm) &
   ½-inch (13mm)

Badger filbert, no. 10

Hake, 1¾-inch (44mm)

OTHER MATERIALS
Robert Warren's Professional
   Clear Medium

Palette knife (for mixing paint and
   adding water shimmers)

Pattern (See page 125)

1. Value Painting (¼-inch [6mm] & ½-inch [13mm] synthetic flats)

Prepare the canvas for the value painting as described on page 12. Use flat black acrylic for the value painting, alternating between the ¼-inch (6mm) and ½-inch (13mm) synthetic flats as needed (see pages 13-17 for value-painting techniques).

Establish the closer and middle distant tree trunks and ruffle in the foliage using the foliage stroke or the corner of the brush. Control the values of the black acrylic to create different values of gray. Establish the most distant tree line with a vertical scrub and add reflections.

Define the top profile of the mountains with less paint to create a gray outline. Emphasize black to gray shadows following the pattern contours for the proper slopes on the right side of the ridges and peaks. Add a few sloping contours to the left side of the ridges.

Add underwater rock shapes by outlining and adding underline shadow. Create rocks that appear smaller in the distance and become larger as you paint closer to the foreground. Define their shadow sides with black. Add gray values to their lighter sides. Define the stream edges, working in and around the rocks. With vertical broad strokes and horizontal edge strokes, establish dark reflection areas, going over underwater rocks and working between the closer rocks. Add edge shadows to the distant water. Add gray tones to create right and left slopes on the hillsides.

LIGHT BLUE
¼" (6mm) White +⅛" (3mm) Cobalt Blue

LAVENDER-BLUE
½" (13mm) White + ⅛" (3mm) each of Cobalt Blue & Cobalt Violet

PURPLE-GRAY
⅛" (3mm) each of White & Ivory Black & Cobalt Violet

CREAM
½" (13mm) White + a touch of Naples Yellow

2. Sky & Clouds
(No. 10 badger filbert)

Fill in the sky down to the top of the mountains with **Light Blue**. Using **Lavender-Blue**, blot in loose cloud shapes in a diagonal direction, tapering down to the mountains. Blend slightly into the Light Blue.

3. Mountains
(No. 10 badger filbert)

Glaze both sides of the mountains with **Purple-Gray** and clearly define their profiles. Haze the lower areas of the mountains with **Light Blue**, working down to the tree line.

4. Mountains
(No. 10 badger filbert)

Highlight the left sides of the peaks with **Prima Gray**, using the tip of the brush. Emphasize the ridge separating the light and shadowed sides of the mountain peaks. Scoop **Cream** onto the tip of the brush and accent the highlights.

DARK GREEN
¼" (6mm) each of Burnt Umber & Cobalt Blue

MEDIUM GREEN
⅛" (3mm) each Dark Green mix & White & Sap Green & Cobalt Blue

YELLOW-GREEN
⅛" (3mm) each of White & Sap Green

5. Mountain, Tree Line and Tree Line Reflections (No. 10 badger filbert)

Add reflected sky light to the shadowed mountainsides (right sides) with Lavender-Blue. Use Blue-Gray (brush mix **Lavender-Blue** mix + **Purple-Gray** mix + a touch of **Ivory-Black**) to create impressions of the distant tree line. Stroke these in vertically with the chisel edge of the brush. Add corresponding water reflections.

6. Water (No. 10 badger filbert)

Add **Lavender-Blue** to the water areas, using vertical and horizontal strokes. Start below the distant tree reflection area and continue downward right off the bottom of the canvas. Work around the middle rocks and stroke horizontally into the edges of the dark reflections. Let some orange show through. Add **Burnt Umber** to the sides of the water in the foreground. Then glaze over the underwater rocks just enough to give the dry-brushed acrylic a blended appearance while still preserving the rock shapes. Using **Dark Green**, add darker values to the rocky foreground on the lower corners of the canvas. Vertically and horizontally glaze all the tree reflections and under the edges of the rocks on the bank.

7. Water (No. 10 badger filbert)

Add **Bright Blue** (brush mix Light Blue mix + Cobalt Blue) to the middle and closest area of the water. This should be a rich, bright color. Use Light Blue to indicate sky reflections. Use vertical and horizontal strokes, working around the large tree reflections. Create the distant water lines by sweeping into the water from the edges of the trees. As you move to the foreground, soften the blue into the **Burnt Umber** of the underwater rocks. Add **Cream** water shimmers by making a vertical stroke and then zig-zagging through it horizontally. Use thin paint and a light touch, working around and sweeping into the tree reflections.

8. Grass & Trees (no. 10 badger filbert)

Glaze **Medium Green** over the grassy areas on the right and left, working down between the rocks. Also tap this color subtlety into the line of distant trees and onto the right (shadow side) of the middle tree. Add a bit to the corresponding tree reflection. Add a few definite **Dark Green** trunks to the hillside trees. Also add a few darker accents to the tree in the middle of the canvas.

9. Grass & Trees (No. 10 badger filbert)

Add **Naples Yellow** highlight to the grass on the right and left of the painting. Stroke the color in the direction of the land contours, working around the shadows. Using a very light downward tapping of the foliage stroke, add highlights to the middle-tree foliage to suggest leaf clumps. Add horizontal touches of highlights to the tree reflection. Also touch a bit of this color between the dark trunks and foliage of the trees on the right. Add a **Cream** accent to the grassy areas, working around the shadows. Highlight the foliage clumps on the left and center of the middle tree. Add a few **Yellow-Green** strokes between the lights and shadows of the grassy areas, working into the previous colors. Then add a light touch to the center of the middle tree.

10. Trees, Rocks & Bushes (No. 10 badger filbert)

Tap in a **Dark Green** glaze over all the closer trees and bushes on the right and left sides of the painting. Add tree trunks. Establish contrasting dark foliage on the trees against the right grassy area and overhanging into the water on the left, letting the orange canvas show through slightly behind the foliage. Create the profile of the dark rocks on the left against the light water. Use **Medium Green** to define the closer foliage clumps within the masses of foliage you just glazed. Remember to add touches to the bushes.

11. Foliage, Bushes & Trees (No. 10 badger filbert)

Add **Yellow-Green** to the foreground foliage and bushes. Add a few highlights to the Medium Green foliage and a few highlights to the inner foliage clumps. Add a second highlight to the Yellow-Green with **Naples Yellow**. Use **Cream** to add final accents to the backlit left tree edge and to all the highlights of the closer foreground trees and bushes.

12. Tree Foliage (No. 10 badger filbert)

Add slight touches of **Medium Blue** (brush mix Light Blue mix + Lavender-Blue mix) to show reflected sky-color light on the shaded right sides of the middle tree and the left closer tree foliage.

13. Rocks (No. 10 badger filbert)

With the side of the brush, add **Burnt Sienna** in the shadowed areas of a few underwater rocks and to the darker areas of the rocks on the banks. Add a touch of **Prima Gray** to the left side of all the rocks above the water. Create a few new rocks in shadows on the banks. Keep perspective in mind, making the rocks smaller in the distance and larger in the foreground. Add small touches of Prima Gray along the bank and a hint to show rock reflections along the water edge. Use light, loose strokes to add a very thin **Purple-Gray** glaze to the shadow sides of the rocks. Create more rocks of various sizes and add their reflections under the right bank in the water. Add a few touches of this color to suggest more rocks under the foliage in the shadowed areas of both the right and left banks.

14. Rocks & Shimmers (No. 10 badger filbert & palette knife)

Add small touches of **Cream** to selectively highlight the rocks. Keep perspective in mind and avoid the shaded areas. Add **White** water shimmers with a palette knife (see page 20).

15. Water Movement & Rocks (No. 10 badger filbert)

With the edge of the filbert (or another very small brush), cut in a very thin line of **Light Blue** water movement along the banks, working in and out of rocks and cutting under and against them. With a filbert, add a few touches of reflected light to the shaded right sides of all closer rocks above water.

ROCKY MOUNTAIN RIVER

Finishing Touches (Hake)

If necessary, redefine the tree trunks and the bottom shadows of the underwater rocks with **Dark Green**. Then mop the distant trees and the water. (See page 19 for an explanation of mopping.)

Deep Forest Stream

**AS A CHILD,** I enjoyed hiking in the woods and playing in its streams. Occasionally, I'd be drawn by the sounds of a distant waterfall that seemed to be there just for me to find in the sometimes dark and curious forest shadows. When I found the fall, I'd take off my socks and shoes, sit on a mossy rock and stick my toes in the cool, clean water, pausing long enough to enjoy nature's wonders.

This painting offers a lesson in capturing two of nature's more demanding subjects and their relationship to each other: rocks and water. By first locking in the detail with an extensive black acrylic value plan, you can focus on adding beautiful, rich natural colors while keeping the dark values in the water and rock shapes.

materials

SURFACE
Stretched Canvas, 12" × 16"
(30cm × 41cm)

ACRYLIC
Luminous Orange

Flat Black

OIL
Martin/F. Weber Permalba White
- 1¾" (44mm)

Martin/F. Weber Prima Oil Colors
Naples Yellow - ¼" (6mm)
Cobalt Violet - ¾" (19mm)
Cobalt Blue - ¾" (19mm)
Burnt Umber - ¼" (6mm)
Sap Green - ½" (13mm)
Phthalo Green - ⅛" (3mm)
Ivory Black - ⅛" (3mm)
Burnt Sienna - ¼" (6mm)
Cadmium Red Light - ⅛" (3mm)
Prima Pink - ⅛" (3mm)

BRUSHES
Foam, 1-inch (25mm) (to apply
Luminous Orange)

Bristle, 1-inch (25mm)
(to apply medium)

Synthetic flat, ¼-inch (6mm) &
½-inch (13mm)

Badger filbert, nos. 6 & 10

Hake, 1¾-inch (44mm)

OTHER MATERIALS
Robert Warren's Professional
Clear Medium

Palette knife (for mixing paint)

Pattern (see page 126)

1. Value Painting (¼-inch [6mm] & ½-inch [13mm] synthetic flats)

Prepare the canvas for the value painting as described on page 12. Then proceed with flat black acrylic, using a ½-inch (13mm) synthetic flat for larger areas and a ¼-inch (6mm) synthetic flat for more detailed areas (see pages 13-17 for value-painting techniques).

Define all tree trunks. Paint darkest values in the rocks. Fill in dark masses of foliage on the left and right banks and across the distant water edge and rocks. Create low foliage in the middle of the painting and over the trunks on the right side; work around sky's light area. Add darkest areas to water with mostly horizontal strokes, adjusting for the contours above the waterfall and the almost vertical direction of the waterfall. Add dry-brush (gray) strokes to the remaining water area except where the water is lightest. Add dry-brush directional strokes to the remaining areas on tops of rocks, but don't cover all the orange. Allow to dry. Apply clear medium (see page 17).

CREAM	**VIOLET**	**LAVENDER-BLUE**	**DARK GREEN**	**PURPLE-GRAY**	**PEACH**
¼" (6mm) White + a touch of Naples Yellow	¼" (6mm) White + a touch of Cobalt Violet	¼" (6mm) White + a touch each of Cobalt Violet & Cobalt Blue	¼" (6mm) each of Burnt Umber + Cobalt Blue	⅛" (3mm) each of White & Ivory Black & Cobalt Violet	¼" (6mm) White + a touch each of Cadmium Red Light & Naples Yellow

2. Sky (No. 10 badger filbert)

Blot **Cream** into the open space in the sky, using short strokes that cross each other. Blot **Violet** around the edges of the cream, suggesting foliage. Add Violet spots or sky holes to the right and left tree areas.

3. Sky (No. 10 badger filbert & hake)

Blot and scrub very thin **Lavender-Blue**, overlapping the Violet. Also open up a few more sky areas and glaze over the trunks and limbs in places. Strive to create a hazy atmosphere. Blend this light area with a hake brush.

4. Foliage, Trunks & Rocks (No.10 badger filbert)

Using a foliage stroke, tap **Dark Green** foliage overlapping a few hazy, distant tree trunks and leaving several loose areas of sky holes. Redefine lower left trunks. Tap into low foliage area above distant rocks and thinly into area where the flowers will be. Glaze very thinly over all the rocks (both dark and light values) and all dark values in the water.

BLUE-GREEN
¼" (6mm) Dark Green mix + ⅛" (3mm) each of White & Sap Green & Cobalt Blue

YELLOW-GREEN
¼" (6mm) each of White & Sap Green

5. Water (No. 10 badger filbert)

Glaze **Medium Green** (brush mix Dark Green mix + Sap Green) over all the dark- and middle-value areas of water, but not the foam. Use **Aqua** (brush mix Lavender Blue mix + Phthalo Green) to add light streaks, distant falls, close falls and the closest water patterns. Scrub a little of the color thinly into the splash area.

6. Water (No. 10 badger filbert)

Add **Lavender-Blue** to the splash area, water streaks and veils of falls. Scrub and dab with your brush and keep the paint thin.

7. Water (No. 10 badger filbert)

Use **Cream** to highlight the splashes and to add curved, falling accents and "sparks" to the top of the falls. Use a light scrubbing action with short "nervous" strokes for the lower splashes. Stretch and taper your strokes for the horizontal accents. Wipe off the brush on a paper towel often and replenish with clean color.

8. Rocks (Nos. 6 & 10 badger filbert)

For this and the next step, use either a no. 6 or no. 10 badger filbert, depending on the size of the rock you're painting.

Add a thin glaze of **Purple-Gray** to the shadow side of rocks. Allow the black acrylic value study at the base of the rocks to show by not putting on too much color. Add **Burnt Sienna** to the tops of all the rocks. Then add **Lavender-Blue** to the tops of the distant rocks only. Use very light touches.

9. Rocks (Nos. 6 & 10 badger filbert)

Add **Peach** accents to the tops of brightest rocks and add just a touch to distant rocks. Add a few spots of **Aqua** (brush mix Lavender-Blue mix + Phthalo Green) to the closest rocks to suggest lichen in the shadows.

Tip: Details can help tie parts of the painting together through color. In this step, the Aqua lichen ties together the rock and water colors.

10. Flowers (No. 10 badger filbert)

Using the tip of your brush and a small foliage stroke, paint clumps of **Cobalt Violet** blossoms in the shadows. Highlight with **Lavender** (brush mix Cobalt Violet and Lavender-Blue mix). Then add a few touches of **Prima Pink**.

11. Trees & Foliage (No. 10 badger filbert)

With **Dark Green**, restate any dark values if necessary in the foliage, low foliage including flowers, between or under rocks and dark values in the water.

Use **Blue-Green** to create lower dimensional clumps of foliage above the distant rocks, referring to the pattern to get an idea of the foliage shapes. Apply this color to the right and left trees, working off the top of the canvas. Add a little to the flower area. Add a few leaves between the rocks and add a vine hanging over the large rock to the right of the waterfall.

Selectively add **Yellow-Green** to create highlights in a few sunlit areas of the foliage painted in this step, including the hanging vines on the right rock.

12. Rocks & Water (No. 6 badger filbert)

Add **Cream** accents to the tops of the rocks on each side of the waterfall and to the larger rock in the distance. Using small touches, apply Cream highlights to add sparkles to the waterfalls and foreground foam. Accent Cream highlights with **White**.

Tip: Learn the relationship of cool colors against warm colors to add more dimension to your paintings. In landscape paintings, dull, cool colors recede and create more distance. Warm colors advance with richness and intensity.

DEEP FOREST STREAM

Finishing Touches (Hake)

Blot the foliage into the shadows only. Horizontally mop the water, but be careful to mop lightly on the splashes so you don't lose the sparkles. (See page 19 for an explanation of mopping.)

Back Harbor Morning

OVER THE COURSE OF SEVERAL YEARS, I've had the opportunity to teach occasional workshops in Maine, both in studios and en plein air. The people I've met there are laid back, hardworking and wonderful to talk with, and they gladly share their delicious lobsters. With my painting friends I've traveled to islands and explored and painted much of Maine's unique rocky coast and picturesque harbors. I'll never forget this calm scene known as Back Harbor, a small inlet near the village of New Harbor and Pemaquid Point. Imagine as you look at the scene the sounds of buoys dinging and seagulls crying. I'm thankful that this book allows me to share with you one of my fondest memories of a place I love.

In this painting the colorful, sunlit lobster boats contrast against the dark shadows of the many rocks and the deep, dark green reflections of the fir trees. Even the preliminary value study in black acrylic is in itself quite striking as it locks down the boat and dock details with dark contrasts of trees and water.

materials

SURFACE

Stretched Canvas, 12" × 16"
  (30cm × 41cm)

ACRYLIC

Luminous Orange

Flat Black

OIL

Martin/F. Weber Permalba White
  - 2 ⅛" (54mm)

Martin/F. Weber Prima Oil Colors

  Naples Yellow - ⅛" (3mm)

  Cadmium Yellow Light
    - ⅛" (3mm)

  Cadmium Red Light - ⅛" (3mm)

  Burnt Sienna - ⅛" (3mm)

  Cadmium Red Medium
    - ⅛" (3mm)

  Cobalt Violet - ½" (13mm)

  Ivory Black - ½" (13mm)

  Cobalt Blue - ½" (13mm)

  Burnt Umber - ½" (13mm)

  Sap Green - ½" (13mm)

  Turquoise - ⅛" (3mm)

  Alizarin Crimson - a touch

BRUSHES

Foam, 1-inch (25mm) (to apply
  Luminous Orange)

Bristle, 1-inch (25mm)
  (to apply medium)

Synthetic flat, ¼-inch (6mm)

Stiff bristle, no. 10

Badger filbert, nos. 6 & 10

Hake, 1¾-inch (44mm)

Liner (See step 12)

OTHER MATERIALS

Robert Warren's Professional
  Clear Medium

Palette knife (for mixing paint)

Wipe out tool

Pattern (see page 126)

1. Value Painting (¼-inch [6mm] synthetic flat)

Prepare the canvas for the value painting as described on page 12. Use flat black acrylic for the value painting (see pages 13-17 for value-painting techniques).

Define the boat windshields, but do not fill them solidly. Define the boat edges, under-lines, rigging and antennae. Shade the sides black to gray, leaving the right sides of the bows light. Paint the inside of the dinghy black (darkest value). Add tiny underlines of the rim and shade the left side of the dinghy. Add reflections of all the boats by sweeping from the bottom edges with a flat broad stroke, emphasizing the "wiggle" or wavy reflections of the side profiles and bows.

Define the dock platforms and shade their edges. Paint the spaces between the rails, braces and ramp posts black (darkest value). Thinly outline the tops of the handrails.

Define the water edge under the rocks. Define the darkest areas of the rocks' top pro-files and the shadows or crevasses between the highlights of the rocks. Drybrush gray tones on the rocks.

Using the corner of a well-loaded brush,

add roughage above the center and right ramps. Work around the lighter foliage clumps and trunk shapes above the right-side ramp. Contrast black tree trunks against the middle- and light-value open area on the slopes of the hillside. Then paint black top foliage with some gray spaces (dry brush) in order to see the dark tree trunks. Silhouette black lacy treetops, leaving a few open holes around the tops. Paint more solid black down to the top of the open area. Paint black trunks through the light open holes on the left side of the point of land. Add sloping trunk shadows in the open area and scrub diagonal gray shadows. Soften the top of the open slope area with gray. Also blot gray values over the empty foliage clumps and across both dock ramp structures.

Mask off the light windshields of the boats with tape or protect them with a palette knife as you paint the water values. Keep perspec-tive in mind with faint water movements on the left, going from the distant water to the horizon. Using thin horizontal edge strokes, paint almost solid dark horizontal water lines against the shoreline, working under the plat-

CREAM	ORANGE	BURNT ORANGE	MAUVE
½" (13mm) White + ⅛" (3mm) Naples Yellow	¼" (6mm) White + a touch each of Cadmium Yellow Light & Cadmium Red Light	¼" (6mm) White + a touch each of Burnt Sienna & Cadmium Red Medium	⅛" (3mm) each of White & Cobalt Violet + a touch each of Cadmium Red Medium & Ivory Black

(Left) Detail of boats. (Below) Detail of dinghy.

forms, between the boats, and carefully around the dinghy. With thicker lines, create vertical areas of dark reflections just to the right of the front boat and at the bottom of the canvas. Leave a light area under the dinghy and a dark area on the right side of the canvas. Sweep or taper the close, darker water movements into the boat reflections, tapering toward the left off the bottom of the canvas.

Allow the black acrylic value painting to dry. Apply Professional Clear Medium as described on page 17.

2. Sky & Water Reflection (No. 10 stiff bristle brush)

From the center of the canvas to the right, fill in the sky with **Cream** down to the treetops. Then apply this color in horizontal strokes to the lower half of the water on the left. Apply **Orange** to the sky, overlapping the Cream and painting almost to the left edge of the canvas. Moving to the water again, overlap the Cream as you apply the Orange, using horizontal strokes and working up. With **Burnt Orange**, overlap the left side of the Orange in the sky and paint lower down to the water. Add horizontal strokes starting two to three inches (5 to 8cm) below the horizon line and working up toward the horizon line in the water.

PURPLE-GRAY
⅛" (3mm) Cobalt Violet +
a touch each of White &
Ivory Black

BLUE-GRAY
⅛" (3mm) Ivory Black +
a touch each of White &
Cobalt Blue & Cobalt Violet

DARK GREEN
¼" (6mm) each of Burnt
Umber & Cobalt Blue

MEDIUM GREEN
⅛" (3mm) White + a touch
each of Dark Green mix &
Sap Green

YELLOW-GREEN
⅛" (3mm) each White &
Sap Green

PALE LAVENDER
½" (13mm) White + a touch
of Cobalt Violet

3. Sky & Water Reflections (No. 10 stiff bristle)

Start applying **Mauve** at the horizon line and loosely mottle upward, blending as you go. Add horizontal dark values working lower from the horizon line and into the lower left water. Repeat the application in the areas of the previous step with **Purple-Gray**, gradually getting darker as you paint down from the sky and up to the horizon line in the water. Touch in a few sky holes in the left trees. Mottle **Blue-Gray** into the low sky. Define the horizon line and then stroke in a few horizontal dark water lines with the same color. If necessary, go back to any previous color to adjust the transition of values and colors.

4. Land (No. 10 badger filbert)

Using **Purple-Gray**, soften and define all the treetops by thinly painting over the black acrylic shapes. Extend and taper into the sky color to create a soft lavender halo effect.

5. Dark Areas (No. 10 stiff bristle)

Using **Dark Green**, glaze over all the foliage, the hillside, the lower rocks and docks, and horizontally over the dark areas of the water, including the dark reflections of the boats. Paint into the treetops, working around sky holes. Keep this glaze extremely thin so you don't lose the orange undertones. Then add a few tree trunks on the left and define the tree profile.

6. Various Details
(No. 10 stiff bristle & no. 10 badger filbert)

Using the stiff bristle brush, add a hazy effect in a few areas of the upper right trees by blotting in an extremely thin glaze of **Blue-Gray** shadow. Using the tip and edge of the no. 10 badger filbert and the same color, define the water edge with thin broken strokes. Add a few hillside slope strokes to create shadows. Also add a few horizontal water lines, from the shore downward about one to two inches (25 to 51mm). Work some of these lines carefully behind and between the boats. Touch a glaze of this color in the boat windows.

7. Various Details (No. 10 badger filbert)

Using the tip and edge of the brush, blot **Purple-Gray** rock impressions on top of the shoreline, on the edges of the dock platforms, and on a few hillside slopes. Also add a few water lines into the same dark water area where you painted **Blue-Gray** water lines. Define the upper tree trunks against the dark upper trees and add several smaller trunk impressions. Define the ramps and handrails. Glaze over the dinghy.

8. Foliage and Water Reflections
(No. 10 badger filbert)

Loosely blot **Sap Green** foliage clump impressions into the dark background trees, adding just color and not detail. Glaze horizontal strokes to the dark areas of the water. Add some of this color to the dark foliage clumps just above the dock ramps.

9. Various Details (No. 10 badger filbert & wipe out tool)

Use the foliage stroke and **Medium Green** to create more clump definition in tree and bush foliage. Add a few hillside slope strokes. Also add this color to the horizontal ripples in the light areas of the water. With a wipe out tool, pick off a few touches of paint to see a little backlight of orange showing through the tree foliage. You can hold the canvas in front of a bright light to find the orange.

10. Various Details (No. 10 badger filbert)

Using **Yellow-Green**, selectively highlight the foliage and add a few slope strokes to the hill. Add light reflections in the water, working outward from the right side of the closer boat and downward from the bottom of the dinghy. With **Naples Yellow**, add a spark of extra light to the brightest foliage and reflections. Highlight a few rock tops on the point of land on the left. Add a few **Burnt Orange** strokes to the slope. Use the same color for a few dim rock highlights. Also add some of this color to the water reflections. Accent the Burnt Orange strokes with Orange.

11. Various Details (No. 10 badger filbert)

Restate the trunks that show against the hillside with **Dark Green**. Using **Dark Aqua** (brush mix Blue-Gray mix + a touch of White), accent the ramps and handrails, the tops of the dock platforms and a few rocks in the shadows on the shore. Define the float and the top edge of the dinghy. Use the edge of the brush for all the Dark Aqua accents and definitions.

12. Boats
(No. 10 badger filbert & liner)

Glaze over the boat windows with **Purple-Gray**. Then shade the sides of the boats and under the roof overhang. Also paint the antennae, either with the edge of the filbert or with a liner brush.

13. Boats & Dinghy
(No. 6 badger filbert)

Using **Bright Blue** (brush mix Cobalt Blue + Turquoise), paint the sides of the nearest boat as pictured. Add reflections. Use **Light Blue** (add **White** to the **Bright Blue** in your brush) to show reflected light in the shadow areas on the railings, the rear edges of both boats, the vertical posts of the cabins and the left side of the dinghy. Highlight the right side of the bow of the closer boat. Add related reflections. Also add the slight shadow line above the windshields and the molding on the lower bow of the closer boat.

14. Boats (No. 6 badger filbert)

Add **Alizarin Crimson** stripes to the bottoms of both boats, letting the color disappear into the shadows. Add a highlight of **Cadmium Red Medium** to the bottom right side of the bows. With **Light Cream** (brush mix White and Cream mix), highlight the boat roofs, rails, and decks; the base of the windshield posts; and the right side of both boats. Accent the reflections. Also accent the bases of the antennae, the dinghy and its float.

15. Water Highlights
(No. 10 badger filbert)

Drag **Pale Lavender** shimmers on the left side of the water. Start on the horizon and continue downward. Work some shimmers into the rocks and space larger shimmers further apart in the lower left water. Accent the very lightest water reflections to the right of the blue boat with Cream. Restate water movements in the dark areas with **Dark Green**.

BACK HARBOR MORNING

Finishing Touches (Hake)

Finish by mopping the water horizontally. Be sure to wipe off the brush between strokes. Also, mop the sky and tree tops. Mop by blotting the darkest areas of the dock areas and trees, being careful not to touch highlights of trees or boats. (See page 19 for an explanation of mopping.)

Patterns

These patterns may be hand-traced or photocopied for personal use only. Enlarge at 200 percent. Then enlarge again at 181 percent to bring up to full size.

GOLDEN OCEAN SUNSET PAGES 22-29

AUTUMN LAKE PAGES 30-37

These patterns may be hand-traced or photocopied for personal use only. Enlarge at 200 percent. Then enlarge again at 194 percent to bring up to full size.

TROPICAL SURF & SHADOWS
PAGES 38-47

WATER LILY POND
PAGES 48-55

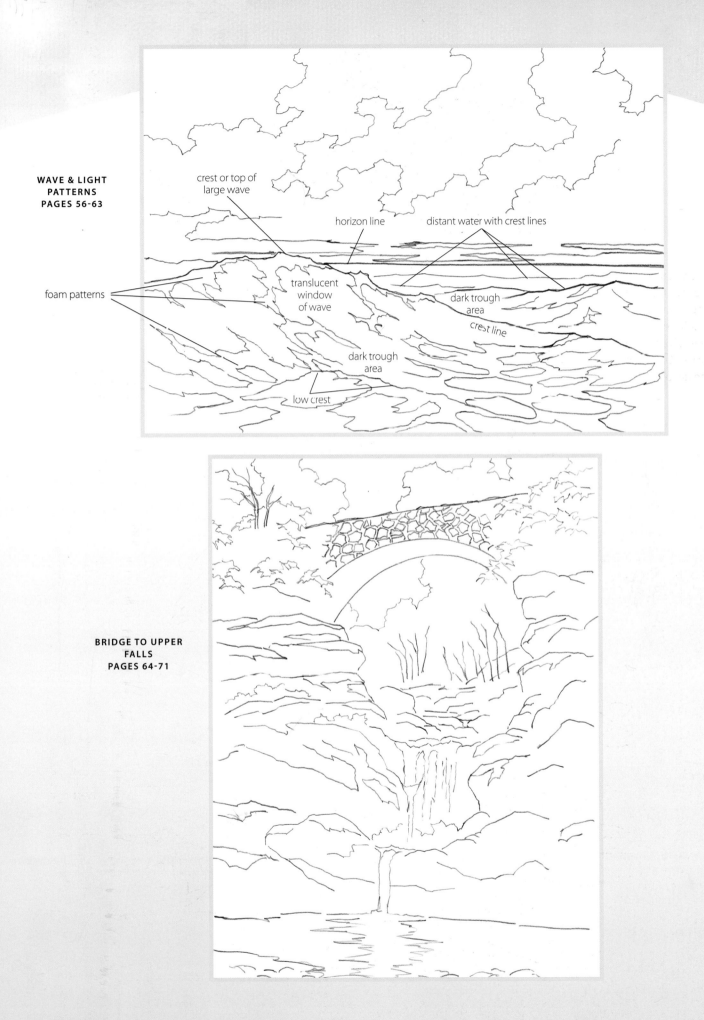

WAVE & LIGHT PATTERNS PAGES 56-63

crest or top of large wave

horizon line

distant water with crest lines

foam patterns

translucent window of wave

dark trough area

crest line

dark trough area

low crest

BRIDGE TO UPPER FALLS PAGES 64-71

These patterns may be hand-traced or pho-tocopied for personal use only. Enlarge at 200 percent. Then enlarge again at 194 percent to bring up to full size.

FLORAL GARDEN REFLECTIONS PAGES 72-79

SNOWY BLUE RUN CREEK PAGES 80-87

**BIG THOMPSON
RIVER CANYON
PAGES 88-95**

**ROCKY
MOUNTAIN
RIVER
PAGES 96-103**

These patterns may be hand-traced or photocopied for personal use only. Enlarge at 200 percent. Then enlarge again at 197 percent to bring up to full size.

DEEP FOREST STREAM PAGES 104-111

BACK HARBOR MORNING PAGES 112-120

Index

The BEST in painting
instruction *and* inspiration is from
North Light Books!

Artist's Photo Reference: Water & Skies

Gather insight and inspiration from more than 470 outstanding reference photos of water and skies in various weather and lighting conditions. Subject matter includes streams, rivers, waterfalls, waves and breathtaking cloud formations. An introductory section gives tips for taking your own photos, and 6 step-by-step demonstrations by several artists show you how to paint scenes based on photos from the book.
ISBN-13: 978-1-58180-165-1, ISBN-10: 1-58180-165-3, paperback, 144 pages, #31919

Painter's Quick Reference: Landscapes

When you're in a hurry for landscape painting help, here's the book to turn to for ideas, instruction and inspiration. With more than 40 step-by-step demonstrations by 21 artists, *Painter's Quick Reference: Landscapes* shows you how to paint all major landscape elements, including clouds, mountains, trees, water and much more. Use this special guide to jumpstart your creativity, learn painting techniques or explore new mediums—including acrylic, watercolor and oil.
ISBN-13: 978-0-58180-814-8, ISBN-10: 1-58180-814-3, paperback, 128 pages, #33495

Painting Landscapes Filled with Light

Capture the rich, illusive properties of light! In 10 step-by-step projects, Dorothy Dent shares her easy-to-master techniques for painting light-filled landscapes in different seasons, weather conditions and times of day. Dorothy's projects include oil and acrylic painting demos, with advice for adapting the technique used for one medium to that of the other. Prepare to be amazed by the landscapes you create!
ISBN-13: 978-1-58180-736-3, ISBN-10: 1-58180-736-8, paperback, 144 pages, #33412

Paint Along with Jerry Yarnell, Volume Seven: Painting Perspective

Let the host of the popular PBS television series, Jerry Yarnell School of Fine Art, take the mystery out of perspective. First learn the principles behind painting accurate and realistic landscapes, buildings and other man-made creations in one-point and two-point perspective. Then apply your knowledge to 7 beautiful step-by-step acrylic painting projects perfect for both beginning and intermediate painters.
ISBN-13: 978-1-58180-379-2, ISBN-10: 1-58180-379-6, paperback, 128 pages, #32394

These books and other fine North Light titles are available at your local art or craft retailer, bookstore or from online suppliers.